AT THE EDGE OF CAMELOT

AT THE EDGE OF CAMELOT

Debating Economics in Turbulent Times

Donald W. Katzner

OXFORD
UNIVERSITY PRESS

OXFORD
UNIVERSITY PRESS

Oxford University Press, Inc., publishes works that further Oxford University's
objective of excellence in research, scholarship, and education.

Oxford   New York
Auckland   Cape Town   Dar es Salaam   Hong Kong   Karachi
Kuala Lumpur   Madrid   Melbourne   Mexico City   Nairobi
New Delhi   Shanghai   Taipei   Toronto

With offices in
Argentina   Austria   Brazil   Chile   Czech Republic   France   Greece
Guatemala   Hungary   Italy   Japan   Poland   Portugal   Singapore
South Korea   Switzerland   Thailand   Turkey   Ukraine   Vietnam

Published by Oxford University Press, Inc.
198 Madison Avenue, New York, New York 10016
www.oup.com

Oxford is a registered trademark of Oxford University Press

Library of Congress Cataloging-in-Publication Data
Katzner, Donald W., 1938–
    At the edge of Camelot : debating economics in turbulent times / Donald W. Katzner.
        p. cm.
    Includes index.
    ISBN 978-0-19-976535-5 (cloth : alk. paper) 1. University of Massachusetts at Amherst.
Economics Dept.—History. 2. Economics—Study and teaching (Higher)—Massachusetts—
Amherst—History.   I. Title.
HB74.8.K38 2010
330.071′174423—dc22   2010033707

9 8 7 6 5 4 3 2 1

Printed in the United States of America
on acid-free paper

For
Erin and Todd
and
Jennifer and Brett

CONTENTS

PREFACE

History, like beauty, is in the eyes of the beholder. This is especially true for someone like me who is not a trained historian. But regardless of background, we can all write about our perceptions, understandings, and interpretations of what we read, what we hear, and what we encounter. It is in this spirit that I present my view of the history of the Economics Department at the University of Massachusetts at Amherst from 1965 to 1981.

It seems to me that the story to be told is extraordinary. Of course, it is not unusual for an academic department to experience a rapid upswing or downturn in accomplished scholarly personnel. But what was unusual about the University of Massachusetts' Amherst Economics Department during the period had three aspects: First there was the speed of changeovers in which an upswing was followed by a downturn and then another upswing all in the space of six short years. Second was the composition of the two upswings in which a visible group of traditional economists containing a future Nobel laureate and a future president of the University of Chicago was put together and then followed shortly thereafter by an even more visible group of radical political economists. The creation of the latter group involved the hiring of the so-called radical package, consisting of five radical political economists. At that time the field of radical political economy focused on economic inequality and imperialism and the conflicts among societal groups relating to them. The ideas of Karl Marx were central in analyzing these and related issues. Although the McCarthy-era investigations of communists in the U.S. government had ended almost twenty years earlier, this was still the height of the Cold War, when the fear of Communism and the Soviet Union was palpable throughout the country. Marxian analysis was considered by many Americans to be both subversive and dangerous, and politicians frequently attacked those who viewed the world through a Marxian lens. Moreover, practically nothing investigated within the field of radical political economy, nor the methodology it employed, was considered to be relevant to economics by the economics establishment. Clearly, then, the hiring of the radical package by a major public university was, by itself, unprecedented. The third unusual aspect was that in spite of the many years of bitter fighting in the Department, especially during the year in which the radicals were hired and throughout their first two years on the University's Amherst campus, radicals and a reconstituted group of more traditional economists were actually able to set aside their differences and create a viable and exciting intellectual community.

Thus, two groups of idealists, the traditional and radical economists, came to the Amherst campus of the University of Massachusetts to create, in the case of the first, something that did not exist at the University, and in the case of the second, something that did not exist anywhere in the world. Both groups ran up against different aspects of the political realities of those turbulent times. The former faced the wrath left over from the Civil Rights and

Vietnam War protest movements on the left; the latter had to deal with the widespread fears of Communism and the Soviet Union on the right. The first group was not successful in adjusting to the challenges it confronted and, as a result, it disappeared. (Although this group was subsequently reconstituted as previously indicated, the reconstituted group held different attitudes and approaches to traditional economics than the group it replaced.) The second group made the necessary accommodations and survived.

To be sure, there were other economics departments in universities scattered around the United States at that time with varying numbers of radical political economists. (Experiences in Economics Departments at the University of California at Riverside, the University of Notre Dame, and the New School for Social Research are briefly noted in Appendix B.) In some cases the numbers were quite small. In others they were large enough to make radical political economics a full-fledged field that became part of the PhD program. But at many universities, the radical political economists on the faculty and the students who wanted to take courses from them had to endure harassment in a hostile environment, and several of the radical political economists even had to face termination. F. Lee, in his *A History of Heterodox Economics*[1] provides considerable detail, and a small portion of that material will be covered in Chapter 4. Nevertheless, the situation in the Economics Department at the University of Massachusetts at Amherst was unique in that it had the largest and most visible group of Marxist economists in any university at the time, and its PhD program was the only one in which the entire thrust of its structure and content was intensely and single-mindedly focused on radical political economy. Even courses like microeconomic theory, one semester of which was required for the

---

1. (London: Routledge, 2009, pp. 68–74)

PhD, were taught as foils against which radical political economics could be compared and could serve as the basis for criticism.

By predilection and training, I am a nonradical or traditional economist. I joined the University of Massachusetts' Economics Department in Amherst in the fall of 1975. During the previous academic year, the first year in which the full complement of radical political economists was in residence, there had been a very difficult struggle in the Department—one of those alluded to earlier—over two tenure cases that had pitted the radical against the nonradical faculty. That battle could be construed as the culmination of many years of hostility and bitter fighting that had existed in the Department. In any case, when I arrived there was calm, but just below the surface tensions were considerable. That year the Department chairman resigned, and because I carried none of the local historical baggage of my colleagues, I found myself thrust into the chair position in the fall of 1976. For the next five years, I was centrally involved in resolving conflicts between the two sides of the Department. Because I was in the middle, at least politically, if not ideologically or intellectually, it seems appropriate that I should try to set out a "balanced" history of the 1965–1981 period.

In the story I am about to tell, there were many heroes. But I do not believe there were any villains. Difficulties, serious and not so serious, arose because of honest disagreements about what was important and what ought to be done. Of course, some felt betrayed and otherwise deeply hurt by others. However, it is not my purpose to deal with such feelings or to settle any scores. I only want to show how circumstances and differences among honorable people led to the remarkable events in the Department of Economics at the University of Massachusetts at Amherst during the years under consideration. As will be described on subsequent pages, throughout the period to which my story directs attention and up to the present, there has been in the Department a remarkable diversity of ideas and extraordinary intellectual stimulation, excitement, energy, and achievement. I consider myself very fortunate to have been a part of it.

In writing this history, I have communicated with many past and present faculty and graduate students on all sides who participated in the fights and other events that occurred, and everyone has been very cooperative in helping me to determine what seems to have transpired. Space limitations do not permit me to acknowledge and thank everyone by name. However, those who have helped the most in this regard, by sitting through long interviews,[2] by providing long written statements, and/or by commenting on early drafts of chapters and/or the entire manuscript include Norman D. Aitken, Dean Alfange Jr., Jack Amariglio, Stephen E. Cullenberg, Michael H. Best, Samuel S. Bowles, James R. Crotty, Gerald Friedman, Marshal C. Howard, Connie Kindahl, Robert Pollin, Cadwell L. Ray, David F. Ruccio, Steven A. Resnick, Anwar M. Shaikh, Hugo F. Sonnenschein, Donald R. Stabile, Douglas Vickers, Richard D. Wolff, and Arthur W. Wright.

I am also grateful to those who have helped by providing me with documents, many of which were written by the principals of my story. In particular, Connie Kindahl gave me access to her late husband James K. Kindahl's extensive personal files relating to his years as head of the Economics Department and to certain matters concerning the Department in subsequent years. Michael F. Milewski located or aided in finding many important documents

2. Some of the problems associated with economists (myself) interviewing other economists have been described by E.R. Weintraub, "History of Thought Introduction: Economists Talking with Economists, An Historian's Perspective," in *Inside the Economist's Mind: Conversations with Eminent Economists*, P.A. Samuelson and W.A. Barnett eds. (Malden, MA: Blackwell, 2007), pp. 1–11.

in the University's library archives. From those same archives, Robert S. Cox provided most of the photographs that appear on subsequent pages. Finally, Arthur W. Wright gave me permission to peruse his confidential tenure and promotion file, and Donna L. Marino in the University administration made the arrangements for me to see it.

What I found in collecting these materials, and what anyone who has done this kind of work already knows, is that memories (including my own) are quite imperfect.[3] We forget events, misinterpret them, modify them from actual occurrences, and add things that did not in reality take place. One person's memory of specific happenings will frequently contradict that of another. I also found that documents are not always clear and often raise more questions than the answers they provide. As a consequence, it sometimes becomes very difficult to determine exactly what actually happened. So in writing this history, I have left out the details of which I am most unsure. I have had to make what seemed to me to be reasonable inferences from documented or remembered events. I have also had to be careful not to violate confidentialities. Thus, there are unavoidable gaps in my story, but I trust not so many and not so wide as to detract from the development and flavor of events. I can only hope the result is worthy of all the help that I have received.

3. A discussion of some of the limitations of relying on memory appears in E.R. Weintraub, "Autobiographical Memory and the Historiography of Economic Thought," *Journal of the History of Economic Thought* 27 (2005): 1–11.

AT THE EDGE OF CAMELOT

Chapter 1

Introduction

Ask ev'ry person if he's heard the story;
And tell it strong and clear if he has not:
That once there was a fleeting wisp of glory
Called Camelot.

A.J. Lerner and F. Lowe, *Camelot*

Economics is an intellectually challenging and socially and cultur-ally significant discipline. It emerged from the shadows of moral philosophy and mercantilism in the eighteenth century to acquire a nascent autonomy in David Hume's *Essays Moral, Political and Literary* (1752) and Adam Smith's *Wealth of Nations* (1776). Its early designation as political economy pointed to its relevance for the state of human affairs and for the wider aspects of social dis-course. As the industrial revolution advanced, businessmen wel-comed what it had to say about the generation of incomes, wealth, and general prosperity. Drawing-room courtesies and conversation embraced its aims and claims, and its practitioners, notable in the case of David Ricardo, acquired seats in the British parliament. Economics, as it came to be called, had become a subject in which laymen needed to take an interest, often making more than a mere dilettantish acknowledgment of it. Its scope and cogency seemed to argue for new possibilities of human good. Its nineteenth-century classical and neoclassical formulations asserted that the structure of social relations was such that the economy would automatically lead to optimum welfare and generalized benefit. However, dissent lay not very far beneath the surface. Methodological revolutions defied accepted and traditional assumptions, and conflicts of explanatory approaches recurred. What economics was doing and what it should be about became matters of sharpening debate.

The conflicts over approaches grew as the twists and cycles of economic prosperity in the late nineteenth and throughout the twentieth century confronted intellectual complacencies. But two propositions became unarguably clear: that economics had something significant to contribute to human welfare, and that some understanding of what the subject involved was a necessary part of a lay person's education.

Along with acceptance of the latter proposition, economics acquired its own respected place among traditional university disciplines. And it was within the university environment that the debates described earlier were most vigorously pursued. Indeed, the hold-over of income and wealth disparities from the industrial revolution, the manner in which the economic aspect of affairs impinged on the state of the poor and relatively disadvantaged, and a recurring concern for the possibility of conflicts between economic and social classes combined to give the subject a heightened diversity of viewpoint and argument.

The chapters that follow will bring to prominence a foremost and uniquely remarkable instance of the approach struggles that have occurred in universities within the economics discipline. The story told will be of interest, not only to those who were caught up in the relevant historical movements, but also to those whose inquisitiveness leads them to explorations of the logic of social and political discourse. For from the mid 1970s through the mid

1980s (of necessity, the present narrative actually begins earlier) the University of Massachusetts at Amherst gave hospitality to one of the most significant experiments in academic cultural change that have occurred in American intellectual history. The issues that story raises bring into focus a recurring question of academic and administrative importance: To what extent is perfection on the levels of administration and scholarship attainable, or even approachable, in an imperfect world? That question raises, of course, others of obvious and even critical significance. For example, what is to be held as the criteria of perfection on the levels in view? And how, on the level of administration, are those criteria to contribute to the wider objectives of university ambience and culture; and on the level of scholarship, what is to determine significance, worthiness, and fitness in the larger scope of learning?

The perfect world, as it appears in Lerner and Lowe's vision of the Arthurian legend, is one in which knights would lay down their arms. Physical force would be employed only for the destruction of evil. Knights would sit at a table that was round (without the head position of a rectangular table) so that all would have equal status, and jealousies would not, therefore, arise. Chivalry and civility would reign supreme, there would be justice for all, and everyone would live happily ever after. Of course, such perfection in any context, is, to the extent that it can be realized, ephemeral and dreamlike. The ideal itself is elusive and illusory, and cannot fully exist among human beings in reality. Shortly after Arthur created his faultless Camelot, human frailties intruded and cracks appeared in it. Those frailties eventually led to its demise.

Academic departments, too, sometimes strive for a perfection that also turns out to be fleeting and flawed. That was certainly the case with the Economics Department at the University of Massachusetts at Amherst during the mid- to late 1970s and early to mid-1980s. But to revert to a question already raised, what precisely was the perfection the Department pursued? And how close did it come to achieving it? One way of answering these questions, and one way of approaching the interpretation of what went on in the Department during the period, is suggested by referring to the conclusions advanced by certain scholars who were concerned with what a university is and what it ought to be doing.

For example, in the middle of the nineteenth century, Cardinal Newman described a university as "...the high protecting power of all knowledge and science, of fact and principle, of inquiry and discovery, of experiment and speculation; it maps out the territory of the intellect."[1] Although Newman thought that the only function of the university was to provide education to its students,[2] and argued that that education should consist of the pursuit of "liberal" as opposed to useful knowledge,[3] his statement can certainly be construed as identifying a substantial part of what goes on at the multifunctional universities that exist today. Many of those universities claim, as does the University of Massachusetts at Amherst, that their primary functions are to engage in knowledge-extending and knowledge-clarifying research, to teach their undergraduate and graduate students, and to provide service to the communities in which they are located. Although the rhetoric that explains these functions often attributes identical importance and weight to each, it is usually the case that research dominates. As George Orwell put it: "All animals are equal. But some animals are more equal than others."[4] And the same emphasis on research is evident in the writings of those who followed Newman.

1. J.H. Cardinal Newman, *The Idea of a University* (New York; Longmans, Green: 1947), pp. 335–336. Originally published in 1852.
2. Ibid., p. xxvii.
3. Ibid., pp. 99–101.
4. *Animal Farm* (San Diego: Harcourt Brace Jovanovich, 1946), p. 118.

4

Thus, almost eighty years later, Abraham Flexner expanded Newman's conceptualization by asserting that the scholars and scientists of a university should be "... conscious of four major concerns: the conservation of knowledge and ideas; the interpretation of knowledge and ideas; the search for truth; [and] the training of students....''[5] He went on to say that at universities, "... fresh streams of thought are constantly playing upon the preserved treasures of mankind,"[6] and "... calm, philosophic reflection can be brought to bear ..." on "... the theoretical consequences of scientific progress."[7] With respect to social science, "The university must shelter and develop thinkers...who...will explore the phenomena of social life and endeavour to understand them."[8] Moreover, "... there is no telling from what source the magic fact or the magic conception will come. The very breadth of the university increases greatly its potential fertility."[9] In short, a university is "... an institution consciously devoted to the pursuit of knowledge, the solution of problems, the critical appreciation of achievement, and the training of men...."[10]

As a final illustration, consider the words of Noah E. Fehl: "There is no other aspect of the nature...of a university that is so essential to an understanding of its unique character as its origin as a guild,... [a] guild of masters and apprentices in the art of learning and the communication of knowledge."[11] Masters and apprentices are engaged in "... the probing of thoughts and the weighing of

---

5. A. Flexner, *Universities: American, English, German* (London: Oxford University Press, 1968), p. 6. Originally published in 1930.

6. Ibid., p. 7.

7. Ibid., p. 18.

8. Ibid., p. 10.

9. Ibid., pp. 33–34.

10. Ibid., p. 42.

11. N.E. Fehl, *The Idea of a University East and West* (Hong Kong: Chung Chi College, 1962), p. 168.

insights and foresights."[12] "Scholarship proceeds by stimulation and inspiration on the level of the masters as well as on that of the students. The master needs those with whom he can think out loud and who can be casually critical and informally helpful just as he needs to hear the thinking out loud of others.... He knows the importance of the day to day exchange of ideas, the benefit of the new angle, the suggestion of a book he had not come across, the fraternal criticism of a judgment where his own competence had blinded him to other alternatives."[13]

These examples suggest that the ideal university is a place where free and open discourse on any intellectual topic, no matter how mundane or outlandish, frequently occurs. Hypotheses, perhaps rather farfetched, are put forward, arguments are pursued, questions are raised, and criticisms, suggestions, and judgments are made. Approaches to the solutions of problems are modified, discarded, and may be reintroduced. Opinions are reversed and may be reversed back to their original forms. The give and take among individuals in such exchanges can be intense and highly stimulating. The greater the diversity of the individuals involved, the more wide-ranging the discussion. Thus the ideal university is an intellectually lively and exciting place.

In today's world, however, universities are too vast and complex to expect much intellectual interaction to occur regularly across academic disciplines. It is more likely that such activity will arise within them. And it is that kind of perfection, consisting of intense intellectual interaction and the considerable stimulation that goes with it, that an academic department might decide to pursue. No doubt there are departments that, to one extent or another, have come close to achieving it.

12. Ibid., p. 170.
13. Ibid., pp. 173–174.

Implicit in this notion of an ideal university is the requirement that the intellectual exchanges just described lead to the development of knowledge and its dissemination. New ideas and approaches are proposed and pursued to the fullest extent possible. When appropriate, they are then published in scholarly journals or books to inform the general academic community and invite it to participate in further discussion. Thus the intellectual interaction on which the notion of perfection is based is a significant part of the research function of the university. And the closer to perfection in this regard a university comes, the more original and deep its research output.

However, the Economics Department at the University of Massachusetts at Amherst in the mid- to late 1970s and early to mid-1980s was special in that the perfection contemplated meant considerably more than this. One way to understand why is to consider the notion of paradigm as introduced by Thomas Kuhn in 1962.[14] A paradigm is a way of viewing and understanding the real world that provides a context for conducting analyses of it. It contains assumptions about the fundamental nature of certain aspects of reality that are considered to be basic and are unquestioningly accepted by adherents to it. And it provides prescriptions for the pursuit of research, including the character of the questions asked, and the approaches taken to answer them. Because, in these terms, the differences between paradigms is so great, cross-paradigmatic discussions and other communication is rather difficult. Moreover, paradigms can neither be compared (because they focus on distinct phenomena or distinct aspects of those phenomena) nor empirically established (because all empirical studies necessarily rest on

---

14. For a more complete summary of Kuhn's argument than that presented here see J. Eatwell, et al, eds., *The New Palgrave*, v. 3 (London: Macmillan, 1987), pp. 795–796. The following presentation is drawn from this material.

the foundation of some paradigm in the first place). Thus, it is possible, for example, to regard classical mechanics, thermodynamics, general relativity, and quantum mechanics as separate paradigms in the field of physics. Those paradigms complement and coordinate with each other in that each focuses its attention on explaining a different aspect of physical reality.

Now, to the extent that perfection of intense intellectual interaction occurs among the individuals of an academic department, it typically arises within the context of a given paradigm. Assumptions relating to a particular issue may be questioned, issue-specific approaches and arguments may be criticized and challenged, and judgments may be made, but they are all constrained by an accepted vision of the way the world operates, an accepted set of underlying assumptions about that reality, and an accepted overall approach to the pursuit of scholarship in the general field of inquiry. By contrast, the acute and vigorous intellectual interaction in the Economics Department at the University of Massachusetts at Amherst during the mid- to late 1970s and early to mid-1980s occurred across different paradigms.[15] And that gave it a depth and intensity that brought it much closer to the ideal, and that was quite unusual in a university community even when considering, say, the multiple paradigms present in physics mentioned earlier. Although, in the case of physics, the paradigms were, as previously noted, cooperative in explaining physical reality, between 1974 and 1985, no less than four major paradigms could be discerned within the Economics Department that were *competing* among each other to explain the same phenomenon, namely, the workings of the real economic world. Competition arose in that the

---

15. The word *paradigm* is often taken to have a broader meaning than that implied in this context. But because the Economics Department and its faculty used that expression in the narrow sense of identifying the different approaches set out later, it is historically correct to employ the word here.

adherents of each paradigm believed that the approach to reality on which their paradigm focused, and the understandings that emerged from their analyses, provided *the* appropriate way to view and explain economic behavior. It was the rivalry between those paradigms that set the tone of discussion in the Department and imbued it with an unusual life and energy. In this sense, the Department came closer to the perfection previously described than that achieved throughout most American universities.

One of the paradigms represented in the Department, the neo-classical paradigm, was dominant in the economics profession of the time. On the most fundamental level, that paradigm was based on the notion that observations of economic reality are separate from thoughts about that reality. The scholar stands apart from the economic world he is trying to analyze scientifically and explain. The most basic units in that world are taken to be consumers and firms, and all analytical structures in it are constituted from those units. Markets are comprised of individual consumers and firms; the economy is made up by the fusing together of all such markets. Consumers and firms are rational actors pursuing behaviors that are consistent with their self-interests. Markets and the economy as a whole tend toward equilibrium, a position of rest in which there is no tendency for anything to change or any unit to change what it is doing, and in which, as a result, economic reality continuously reproduces itself.

Perhaps the most common particularization of this vision was that of the general equilibrium system that explains the work-ings of the perfectly competitive microeconomy: Consumers are endowed with resources that are sold to obtain income with which to buy commodities. Buying and selling decisions are derived from maximization of appropriately specified objective functions in relation to individuals' preferences. Firms hire inputs to produce and sell outputs, and all production energy is geared to the max-imization of their profit or the economic value of the activity in which they engage. The markets in which all buying and selling activity takes place are themselves perfectly competitive. That is, each has large numbers of small buyers and sellers, a standardized product, free entry into and exit from the market for any unit in the economy, and all market participants know everything there is to know about every commodity and what each participant is doing. The equilibrium in the perfectly competitive economy is usually referred to as "general" equilibrium. This representation of the microeconomy was also thought to be the basis for understand-ing the macroeconomy in relation to what was then known as the "neoclassical synthesis."

Two of the faculty members in the Economics Department who were associated with this paradigm were James K. Kindahl and myself.[16]

The remaining three paradigms all fell within the field referred to as radical political economy. This multiparadigmatic field, as it existed in the 1970s and 1980s, grew out of interest in the study of economic inequality and imperialism.[17] Because neoclassical eco-nomics had little to say on these subjects that was not considered to be either unsatisfactory or apologetic, economists interested in them turned to the writings of Karl Marx and other nonorthodox economists.[18] Although there is no succinct generalization that can

16. It should be noted, however, that Kindahl was an empirical economist who had little inter-est in economic theory per se.
17. Because inequality and imperialism were considered by radical political economists to be breakdowns of the economic order, radical political economics could be viewed as an example in a different context of J.M. Keynes' response to the malfunctioning of the econ-omy as a whole. See his *The General Theory of Employment, Interest and Money* (London: Macmillan, 1936).
18. J. Eatwell, et al., eds., *The New Palgrave*, v. 4 (London: Macmillan, 1987), p. 36.

fully describe the field of radical political economy in its entirety, one central characteristic

> ...is the premise that there are conflicts of power and interests between groups and classes in society and that the dominant groups exercise determining influences on economic thought as well as on economic activity. The economy is viewed as part of a socio-cultural system; it is formed by this system, but at the same time influences culture and society. [Thus any]...understanding of economic phenomena can only take place...[from an interdisciplinary perspective]. When the economy is viewed in this way, a major role is given to institutions in the determination of economic life.[19]

Another focal point is the idea that history plays a substantial role in the shaping of actual conflict and institutions, and is another significant determinant of current economic life. Thus, conflict, institutions, and history lie at the core of radical political economics. Because conflict and inequality are also important issues in the labor movement, the frequent interaction between radical economists and labor unions is not surprising. Sometimes, following the practice in the Economics Department at the time, the word *radical* will be dropped and the field will be referred to as simply "political economy."[20] Alternatively, the term "radical economics" will occasionally be employed. Economists (and students) whose work is primarily associated with that field will often be called radical economists (or students), or just radicals for short.

---

19. P. Arestis and M. Sawyer, eds., *The Elgar Companion to Radical Political Economy* (Aldershot: Elgar, 1994), pp. xii–xiii.
20. This usage of the term "political economy" should not be confused with that employed at the inception of economics as an independent discipline (recall p. 1 earlier). See also, for example, P. Arestis and M. Sawyer, eds., op. cit., p. xii.

A second paradigm, one of the three political-economy paradigms and identified in the Economics Department with the names of Samuel S. Bowles and Herbert Gintis (among others), took the same position concerning the separation of reality and thoughts about it as the neoclassical paradigm. Also in confluence with that paradigm, methods of analysis were to be scientific in that ideas could be formalized and checked, at least in principle, against reality. But it departed from the neoclassical paradigm in its association with both Marxism and political and social liberalism. Indeed, Marxian thought, having to do with the workings of reality in terms of dialectical materialism, and liberalism as it bore on freedom, democracy, and individual rights, provided the context within which the economy was understood and studied. The issues fundamental to that study, in contrast to those of the neoclassical paradigm, related to the role of collective action and conflict among groups in bringing about change, the dynamic and endogenous quality of preferences and technologies, the nature of employment as a struggle between relatively powerless employees and considerably more powerful employers, and the historically specific character of capitalism.

The third paradigm linked to James R. Crotty and partly to Leonard A. Rapping (at least during his early years at the University of Massachusetts) assumed the identical stance concerning the importance of scientific analysis and the separation of reality from thoughts about it. But it was concerned with the macroeconomy as a whole rather than with the individual units that comprise it. Insights into the workings of the macroeconomy were drawn from the writings of Marx that had to do with the reserve army of the unemployed, the role of money, finance, credit, and so on. These elements were combined with the ideas of Keynes,[21] not those translated and

21. For example, J.M. Keynes, "The General Theory of Employment," *Quarterly Journal of Economics* 51 (1937): 209–223; and *The General Theory of Employment, Interest, and Money* (New York: Harcourt Brace, 1936).

transported by Hicks[22] and others into what was referred to earlier as the neoclassical synthesis, but rather those that could not be fitted into that synthesis and were left behind by it. Emphasis on the latter led to a conceptualization of Keynesianism that differed from the Keynesian component of the neoclassical synthesis in its theoretical structure, methodology, and policy prescriptions. It included, for example, the notions that the future is unknowable, even probabilistically, and that decisions made now that affect it are largely irreversible. The macroeconomic issues of unemployment, price stability, and economic growth were approached from these perspectives, and the vision of the operation of the macroeconomy implied by them was quite different from that obtained through the lens of the neoclassical paradigm.

Another aspect of this latter difference arose from the fact that, up through the early 1970s, the traditional approach within the neoclassical paradigm assumed that macroeconomic models were built up from the microeconomic general equilibrium system described earlier.[23] It was not until the late 1970s that economists began to realize that this might not be the appropriate or most productive procedure.[24] But in moving away from the general equilibrium system as a base, macroeconomics was still thought to be founded on microeconomic ideas. However, the Crotty-Rapping paradigm viewed macroeconomics as primary and microeconomic structures as dependent on the state of the macroeconomy.

The last paradigm, represented in the Economics Department by Stephen A. Resnik and Richard D. Wolff, was based on an interpretation of Marxian analysis that rejects the separation (present

22. J.R. Hicks, "Mr. Keynes and the 'Classics;' a Suggested Interpretation," *Econometrica* 5 (1937): 147–159.
23. For example, K.J. Arrow, "Samuelson Collected," *Journal of Political Economy* 75 (1967): 730–737.
24. See E.R. Weintraub, *Microfoundations* (Cambridge: Cambridge University Press, 1979).

in the other three paradigms) of economic reality from thoughts about it.[25] Everything in actuality— physical, social, mental, and so forth—is assumed to interact in a mutually constitutive manner with everything else. No economic phenomenon can be understood by detaching it from the milieu of all other economic and noneconomic things and events, including the mental processes of the scholar who is attempting to understand it. The development of these ideas led to what Resnick and Wolff referred to as "overdetermination." Variables, relations, and systems can all be employed to analyze and understand economic reality, but they cannot stand independently on their own. In conducting an economic analysis, such things as the purposes and limits of the analysis, the time interval to be covered, the language, and rules of reasoning are all determined as part of the analysis. And no economic event has a single cause or essence that accounts for its occurrence. To explain the presence of an event—for example, the transition from feudalism to capitalism in Western Europe between 1100 and 1500 AD—requires the recognition of the multitude of mutually interactive elements that led to its being and the homing in on those elements that seem to be most significant.

The starting point for all analyses that fall within this paradigm is the notion of economic class. The latter is defined as that relationship among people in which individuals working for others, that is workers, create surplus value, or the amount by which the value of goods and services produced by those workers exceeds the value the workers are paid.[26] The analyses themselves "... focus

25. A more detailed statement of the philosophical and methodological aspects of this paradigm, and the material from which the following summary is, in part, drawn, may be found in D.W. Katzner, *Time, Ignorance, and Uncertainty in Economic Models* (Ann Arbor: University of Michigan Press, 1998), pp. 18–24.
26. R.D. Wolff and S.A. Resnick, *Economics: Marxian versus Neoclassical* (Baltimore: Johns Hopkins University Press, 1987), p. 17.

Table 1.1

Paradigm	Names Identified in the Text
Neoclassical	Katzner, Kindahl
Marxism combined with political and social liberalism	Bowles, Gintis
Marxism combined with Keynesian macroeconomics	Crotty, Rapping
Marxism as the mutual interaction of all analytical elements	Resnick, Wolff

on the class aspects, class causes, and class consequences of social life"[27] and, not unlike the previously described paradigms in which Bowles and Gintis and Crotty and Rapping worked, they covered such topics as labor power, capital accumulation, economic crises, and imperialism.

The four paradigms are listed in Table 1.1 along with the aforementioned names of the faculty members identified with them.

Another matter relating to the presence of the four paradigms set out earlier deserves mention. In the academic economics profession, there was (and still is) a strong establishment of economists, mostly in the major academic departments, that tightly controlled the intellectual content appearing in the articles of most economics journals and whose views were accepted by most individuals in most economics departments. This control consisted of the setting of fairly narrow rules that defined the limits of acceptable research in the field. Among other things, those rules identified the kinds

27. Ibid, p. 21.

of questions that were worth asking along with the nature of the techniques that could be used to answer them. Of course, rewards (*e.g.*, journal articles published, promotions, etc.) usually went only to those who successfully followed the rules. But during the 1970s and 1980s those rules excluded many of the issues raised and analyses conducted within the three paradigms of (radical) political economy. Thus, the establishment rules determining acceptable creative work could not be applied to much of the research output of the University of Massachusetts Economics Department.[28] In that department, then, publication in nonestablishment approved venues was, of necessity, both considered to be adequate and rewarded. The absence of establishment rules meant that the faculty, including those who worked in the neoclassical paradigm, had unprecedented freedom to choose the directions in which their research progressed. This openness within the Department was a significant contributor to the intellectual creativity and excitement among its faculty and students.

Clearly, individuals who represented any one of the four major paradigms appearing in the University of Massachusetts Economics Department viewed the operation of the economic world in vastly different terms from those who subscribed to the others. And this, in turn, led to remarkably deep, highly intense, enormously stimulating, and always lively discussions concerning various economic issues. These discussions took place among faculty members either directly or indirectly through their students, among students, and between faculty and students. The questions at issue were not of the same kind as, for example, "Should decision-makers' preferences that are taken as given be assumed to have this or that property?"

---

28. From here on, the phrase "at Amherst" is often dropped from the University of Massachusetts at Amherst for expositional convenience.

Rather, they were more on the order of "Do preferences that are given have any relevance at all to the problem at hand?" There is no doubt that the first type of question is important within the context of the paradigm within which it was raised. But the second type arises on a much more fundamental level.

To illustrate these kinds of interactions, consider my own experience in teaching graduate microeconomic theory from the neoclassical paradigm. Between the fall of 1975 and the mid 1980s, I taught two courses in this area each year, one a course required for the PhD degree in the traditional theory of the consumer, the firm, and markets, and the other an optional course in the theory of general equilibrium. Often a radical faculty member would criticize an aspect of microeconomic theory in a graduate course he was teaching. Frequently the students in his course were simultaneously taking graduate microeconomic theory from me and, in my class, those students would ask me about the criticism. I would respond by answering the criticism, and they would report back to their radical instructor. A rejoinder would be communicated back to me again through the students, and the discussion would go on.

In addition, with their mostly nontraditional backgrounds and interests in radical political economics, the questions the graduate students asked in my classes were generally, from my vantage point as a traditional economist, important, interesting, and unlike any I had ever heard before. For example, the students who, in spite of their lack of interest,[29] still knew that, as economists, they had to have some acquaintance with neoclassical economics, could not, coming from their mostly radical perspectives, understand why

29. The graduate students had come to the University of Massachusetts to study radical political economy, not traditional economics.

any economist should be concerned with the questions of existence, uniqueness, and stability of equilibria, either in reference to a system of equations depicting an isolated market or with respect to a model of the economy as a whole. To a mathematician there is no issue here: The purpose of mathematics is to explore the properties of formal structures and their implications, and the questions of existence, uniqueness, and stability of equilibria clearly fall within this realm. The purpose of economics, however, is to explain certain real world phenomena, and the manner in which those questions are related to such reality was not obvious.

Of course, I was quite familiar with the mathematics of existence, uniqueness, and stability issues. But, as someone who received his graduate education from mathematically trained economists in a standard economics department, and who, as a teacher and scholar having already taught in a number of such departments, I had never been asked about and had never given much thought to the methodological importance and significance of those issues. That had simply never come up in my experience; such things having always, as purely mathematical matters, been taken for granted. The same seemed to be true of many of my former colleagues. And so I was forced to confront some fundamental matters that lie at the heart of what economics is and how it goes about explaining economic phenomena.[30] I found all this to be fascinating and remarkably stimulating. Thus, for me personally, the presence of the radicals contributed to an unusual intellectual excitement and intensity that I fully enjoyed and from which I learned a great deal.

---

30. The reason the questions of existence, uniqueness, and stability of equilibria are of vital importance to economists is that the notion of equilibrium provides, in many circumstances, the only link between the economist's explanation of what is going on and the actual thing that is being explained. See D.W. Katzner, *An Introduction to the Economic Theory of Market Behavior: Microeconomics from a Walrasian Perspective* (Cheltenham: Elgar, 2006), pp. 21–22, 336–338, 381–383.

These examples suggest the depth and intensity of discussion and questioning, and the stimulation and learning it provoked, that went on in the Economics Department in the mid 1970s through the mid 1980s. It is in this sense that the Department came very close—indeed, closer than most departments—to the notion of perfection described earlier.

The research output that emerged from this environment was both significant and extensive. Its significance lay in the challenge it presented to the neoclassical paradigm dominant at the time. Issues were raised, such as the power of some individuals over others within the firm, unemployment as a means of disciplining labor, and the endogeneity of preferences, that were thought to reside outside the boundaries of the neoclassical paradigm and that were, in one way or another, eventually co-opted by the establishment and subsequently introduced into a modified version of that paradigm. Extensiveness and a further indication of significance were suggested in a paper by Davis and Papanek who found that, with respect to numbers of citations in journals and books of published work by faculties as listed in the Social Sciences Citation Index and averaged over 1978 and 1981, the University of Massachusetts Economics Department ranked twenty-fourth among 122 PhD-granting institutions.[31] When controlling for the age of faculties, that rank rose to nineteenth.[32] This is rather astonishing given that, as pointed out earlier, many journals at the time (including those thought by the establishment to be most important) would not publish political-economy-type work produced by the Department and that, even when published, many economists simply ignored it. One can only guess at the extent to which the reputation of the

31. P. Davis and G.F. Papanek, "Faculty Ratings of Major Economics Departments by Citations," *American Economic Review*, 74 (1984): 227.
32. Ibid., 228.

Department within the economics establishment would have been improved if the kind of political economy in vogue at the University of Massachusetts had been accepted and vigorously pursued by the economics establishment and its journals.

As has been indicated, the followers of the four major paradigms in the Economics Department saw the functioning of the economy in starkly contrasting terms. Those differences, moreover, extended to the operation of the Economics Department itself, especially in relation to graduate students in their roles as both students and teaching assistants. It turned out that the radical economists from the three non-neoclassical paradigms were all united on this issue with a view that was quite distinct from that of the adherents to the neoclassical tradition. On the one hand, the latter perceived the education process in terms of the master-apprentice relation described in the writings of Fehl, mentioned earlier. Because of their greater experience and more extensive knowledge, the role of the faculty is to lead, whereas that of the graduate student as student and teaching or research assistant is to follow. Combining this with the fact that the faculty has a much longer-term interest in the Department itself, it is the faculty, and only the faculty, who should be making departmental decisions. The position of the radical faculty and graduate students, on the other hand, was expressed by Bowles and Gintis in their *Schooling in Capitalist America.*[33] To prepare students for participation in democratic society and economic life, the educational system needs to be egalitarian and liberating (p. 14). And to achieve this, the educational process has to be democratic, with students and teachers sharing power in pursuing their common interests and in resolving conflicts that arise among them (p. 287). This meant that, at least at the graduate level, students would participate

33. New York: Basic Books, 1976.

in the making of departmental decisions affecting them and their education. Not only were they to participate in determining the requirements and other particulars of the PhD program in which they were enrolled, but they were also to participate in such matters as the hiring of new faculty, the admission of new graduate students, and the assignment of teaching assistants to courses that employed them. In parallel with the intense discussions in the Department on economic matters, then, there often arose equally intense, if not more intense, interactions among graduate students and faculty, and within the faculty itself on questions relating to the actual operation of the Economics Department and its PhD program.

Some might interpret the presence of such debates between graduate students and faculty in the making of departmental decisions as a flaw in the process of pursuing the perfection toward which the Economics Department was striving—a necessary evil, perhaps, that detracted from any attained degree of perfection. But that flaw can also be regarded as a desirable and important part of the near-perfection achieved, without which life in the Economics Department would be considerably less interesting, stimulating, and lively. Regardless, engaging in such debates was a significant portion of the process whereby faculty from the different paradigms learned to live together and, at least to some extent, to benefit from a cross-fertilization of ideas and academic interests.

It is also possible to identify what might be considered flaws that emerged in Departmental organization. First, the heartfelt differences on educational matters among faculty members and between some students and faculty made it necessary to spend long hours working out special procedures for the functioning of the Department. Thus the Economics Department was overadministered in the sense that it had to engage in certain activities (including negotiations as well as the activities that were required as a consequence of the outcomes of those negotiations) to a degree that more typical departments would automatically avoid. Second, intense interactions among people with deep-seated and dissimilar views always has the potential to result in hurt feelings and disruptive behaviors generated by those feelings. Although Department members were generally quite sensitive to this problem and usually took great care to avoid it, there were times when conflicts arose that had to be dealt with. The presence of such flaws, of course, is a consequence of the humanness of our existence, and is one of the reasons why only near perfection, and not full perfection, can be achieved in reality.

Thus, from the mid 1970s to the mid 1980s, the University of Massachusetts Economics Department was home to a group of very bright and energetic scholars who, at the deepest philosophical level, raised fundamental questions about what constituted economics and how economics should be done. They searched for and, to some extent, found distinct, interesting, and sometimes exciting and provocative answers. That is priceless at a university and does not occur very often. Moreover, by its very nature, it is unlikely to last as the world and its priorities change and as a younger generation with different backgrounds and new curiosities replaces the older one.

But there are other levels on which the radical presence may be viewed and understood. The study of radical hires in Economics at the University of Massachusetts also brings into focus the professional, academic, and personal relations that developed from a mixture of disparate intellectual disciplines in an important scholarly environment. In addition, the experiment in creating space for radical political economics that took place served, no doubt, objectives of academic freedom and a certain unfettered right of scholarly inquiry. In examining the unique history involved from those vantage points, a still further contribution may be made to some aspects of the sociology of knowledge. That field of study, of course, is primarily concerned with the ways in which human thought—in the present case academic scholarship—emanates from and is flavored by sociocultural contexts on the one hand, and feeds back on social and cultural structures and experience on the other. In this regard, the significance of the University of Massachusetts experiment rests to a considerable extent on the fact that it provides an important case study of precisely those relations. Upon their arrival in the Economics Department (and to a lesser degree before), the radicals developed thought systems that had been parented by social and cultural events and concerns; and from the perspectives that informed their work and their scholarly contributions, they exerted influence on a variety of sociocultural phenomena. Thus, for example, and as will be set out in detail later, the civil rights and Vietnam War protest movements played an important role in the development of radical thought. And, as described earlier, the work of Bowles and Gintis on education had a significant impact on the relations between graduate students and faculty in the Economics Department.

Answers to the questions of how the group of radical economists at the University of Massachusetts was put together and why it was possible to do so are, as will be seen, remarkable enough. But the coming of the radicals to the University was preceded by the creation in the same Economics Department of a first-rate and important group of active neoclassical economists who were, in part, leaders in introducing mathematics and mathematical statistics into economics, generally, and in what was then the newly emerging more abstract field of mathematical economics.[34] This latter group

34. Later on, after mathematics had infiltrated much of economic analysis, mathematical economics ceased to exist as a distinct field and the standard fields like microeconomic theory maintained their identity as fields but with heavy use of mathematics.

rose in an obscure faculty that had produced little in the way of published research over a long period of time, and did so in the brief space of two years. However, the group of neoclassical economists remained intact for only two more years and, within two years of the departure of its leaders, the vastly different group of radical economists described earlier took their place. In the process of replacement, some of the neoclassicals stayed on and several new ones were brought in. It is rather unusual, of course, for any department to be so successfully built and so successfully reconstituted in such a striking way over such a short span of time. In any case, the story of how the radicals came to the University of Massachusetts and in so doing replaced a highly regarded group of neoclassical economists, and how the representatives of the four paradigms managed to overcome many of their deep-seated differences to form a cohesive department that achieved an unusual degree of near perfection, is fascinating. In the words of L.S. Lifschultz,[35]

> ...the process... [involved, in part,] a most unusual series of events, exceptional within the traditions of American academia for the unparalleled conflict which developed and the clarity of academic principles which finally emerged. The web of events... [included two] attempt[s] to fire a popular teacher,... forceful student protest[s], the resignation of two consecutive Department chairmen,... the assumption of Departmental authority by a dean of the University, and the unprecedented appointment of five radical economists.

The full story will be told in some detail on the following pages, and a time line of major events appears in Appendix A. But before

35. "Could Karl Marx Teach Economics in America?" *Ramparts* 12, no. 9 (April, 1974), p. 30.

turning to the story itself, it is first necessary to consider the historical background that sets the stage for the radical presence. That background includes the evolution of the University of Massachusetts as a university with an environment in which a significant number of radical economists could be hired and prosper; the civil rights and the Vietnam War protest movements that contributed to the university's radical-friendly environment and spawned many radical scholars in general and radical economists in particular; the rise and fall of the economics profession in the public mind and the profession's marginalization of those, including the radicals, who would not confine their attention to the narrow lines of thought approved by the economics establishment; and the development of the Economics Department on the Amherst campus of the University of Massachusetts as a significant force within the neoclassical paradigm of that establishment.

Chapter 2

A Short History of the University of Massachusetts

As is no doubt the case with many public institutions of higher learning, state-level politics has played a major role in the history of the University of Massachusetts.[1] The University began its life as Massachusetts Agricultural College in Amherst toward the end of 1867. The political climate in which that College came into existence was heavily influenced by Jacksonian democracy—the idea that all citizens (not just the wealthy) should have equal political power—and the reform activity (such as the efforts to eliminate restrictions on voting rights) that came with it. One of the targets of the reformers was education. The instruction provided by the private colleges at the time, that is, the classical college curriculum based on the study of philosophy, theology, natural history, mathematics, Latin, Greek, and Hebrew, seemed neither appropriate nor relevant for the purpose of enabling the children of farmers and mechanics to take their place in American society. To achieve the latter, a more utilitarian type of education was needed, one that imparted knowledge of the more practical arts and sciences. That education would

1. The story of the University of Massachusetts up to 1960 presented here is based on H.C. Cary, *The University of Massachusetts: A History of One Hundred Years* (Amherst: University of Massachusetts, 1962). The history for the period 1960–1970 is derived from R.M. Freeland, *Academia's Golden Age: Universities in Massachusetts, 1945–1970* (New York: Oxford University Press, 1992).

require a curriculum that would also include such potentially useful subjects as political economy (in the sense employed when economics was emerging as a separate discipline—recall p. 1), geography, American history, French, and Spanish. Although some private institutions had begun to add instruction in several of these areas, it was not nearly enough. After all, the private institutions catered to the social elite, and the cost of the education they provided was more than most families could afford.

In the forty or so years before the creation of Massachusetts Agricultural College, and in response to pressures coming from various groups, a number of proposals were made for organizing and founding in Massachusetts public institutions of higher learning that would concentrate on instruction in the more practical fields. Some proposed institutions were to offer programs that focused primarily on agriculture; others were to provide a more general curriculum. But although prior to 1867 the Massachusetts legislature issued two charters for agricultural institutions, no public money was allocated for this purpose, and the efforts to establish the schools failed.

It was not until the Morrill Act was passed by Congress and signed by President Abraham Lincoln on July 2 of 1862 that public money became available to support public higher education in Massachusetts. The Act gave to each state 30,000 acres of federal land for each congressman from that state. This land was to be sold to provide the funding for at least one college in the state that would emphasize (not to the exclusion of other scientific and classical subjects) agriculture and the mechanical arts. The institutions formed under the Morrill Act became known as land-grant colleges. The Massachusetts legislature responded to the Morrill Act and the growing public pressure for public higher education by issuing a charter to create Massachusetts Agricultural College on April 28,

1863. The legislation was signed by Governor John A. Andrew the following day, and a Board of Trustees was assigned the task of establishing the college.

Massachusetts Agricultural College had financial difficulties right from the very beginning. Although it did receive funding through the Morrill Act for the purchase of land, and a modest annual income from a trust fund also created under the Morrill Act, those monies were hardly sufficient. The legislature had required that the community in which the College was to be located should be responsible for covering the expense of constructing the buildings. The state would not commit itself to firm financial support, although it did provide two loans before the College opened in the fall of 1867.

Five Massachusetts towns vied to become the seat of the new institution: Lexington, Springfield, Chicopee, Northampton, and Amherst. Amherst was chosen by the Board of Trustees for at least three reasons: (1) the nationally known and very active Hampshire County Agricultural Society was centered in Amherst and was already facilitating considerable interaction between agriculturalists and educators; (2) Amherst was far enough away from urban centers that the experience of students in attendance would be purely agricultural (interaction with the local farm community was anticipated) and not influenced by city life; and (3) housing in Amherst and the libraries and museums of Amherst College were nearby and accessible.

Land for both the campus and a farm was purchased from six Amherst land-owners in October of 1864. The Town of Amherst raised the necessary money for the buildings through taxation and private subscription. After a prolonged dispute within the Board over the campus layout, over which the first president of the College, Henry F. French, resigned, construction was well underway. A curriculum involving agriculture and horticulture (which were to be based on the natural sciences), mathematics, English grammar, modern languages, and the social sciences was approved. A faculty of four, consisting of William S. Clarke (botany and horticulture), Levi Stockbridge (farm superintendent), Henry H. Goodell (rhetoric and modern languages), and Ebenezer S. Snell (mathematics), was hired. Massachusetts Agricultural College opened its doors to 36 male students on October 2, 1867, with Clark, in addition to his professorial duties, as its third president. Late arrivals expanded the class to 56. That first class graduated with Bachelor of Science degrees in July of 1871.

A typical day for the incoming class consisted of mornings with three lectures and recitations, and an afternoon of labor on the farm. Saturday afternoon was set aside for recreation and scientific excursions, and Sunday was reserved for required attendance at church and a Bible class. Academic subjects were not covered in great depth due to the limited time available. And the many demands placed on the faculty deprived them of the time necessary to expand and deepen their intellectual capabilities and offerings—although some significant experimental discoveries that benefited Massachusetts agriculture were made.

Political activism among students at the University of Massachusetts dates to the first class that entered Massachusetts Agricultural College. On two occasions during the course of its four-year tenure the student body went on strike. In one instance, when the heat of the day rose to 100°F in the shade, the class refused to march to the Amherst College chapel. In the other, it protested against the manual-labor requirement. The latter incident led to a heated confrontation between the students and President Clark that was eventually resolved by a compromise in which manual labor would be limited to "educational lines."

During the fifteen years after the entry of its first class, Massachusetts Agricultural College struggled to survive. Educators, still largely sympathetic to the classical curriculum, were dismissive of the new applied approach to science, and they accused the school of having low standards. Farmers were not convinced that academic study was the best way to learn the techniques of farming and farm management. The state legislature, which was expecting the College to be self-supporting, became critical when that proved to be impossible. The state did provide funding for new construction, and it did, however grudgingly, eventually cover the College's debts. However, it remained firm in its unwillingness to commit itself to annual support for the purpose of meeting operating expenses.

These were difficult times for the College. Revenues from the trust fund created by the Morrill Act were shrinking. A library, and more classrooms and laboratory equipment were desperately needed. Enrollments began to decline in the early 1870s, reaching the point at which the incoming class numbered less than twenty students in 1875. Many potential enrollees could not afford the $1,000 four-year tuition, and money was not available for scholarships. In addition, charges of mismanagement, misuse of funds, poor student food, and lax disciplining of students were leveled against the College.

By 1880 the tide had begun to turn. A proposal by Governor Thomas Talbot to close Massachusetts Agricultural College as a public institution and give it to Amherst College was dropped. The College began to receive recognition for the successful experimental work it had done during the 1870s that had made significant contributions to Massachusetts agriculture, and money to fund an experimental station on campus was appropriated by the legislature in 1882. Some additional money for new buildings and scholarships was also provided. At last, the state had committed itself to public support of Massachusetts Agricultural College. New staff was hired and enrollments began to grow. The future of the college was now reasonably secure.

In 1886, Henry H. Goodell, a professor on the original faculty of Massachusetts Agricultural College, was appointed as its president. He remained in that position for nineteen years until 1905. Under his leadership, the College advanced. More new buildings were added, and classroom and laboratory facilities improved. The faculty and student populations continued to expand, and a second Morrill Act, passed by Congress in 1890, provided additional financial support. Although twenty-three years behind the times, the first woman was admitted in 1892. The first Master's degrees were awarded in 1896, and the first Doctor of Philosophy degree in 1902. Goodell himself was personally responsible for transforming the library, with an enormous increase in its collection of books and journals to over 23,000 volumes.

Another student strike shook the campus in 1905. It was provoked by a classroom disturbance that led to the year-long suspension of three seniors. The senior class as a whole apologized to the professor involved. But when the faculty refused to shorten the suspensions, the entire senior class went home. The suspended students were then reinstated, and everyone returned in time to finish up and graduate on schedule.

By 1890, Massachusetts (along with the entire country) was undergoing a rather rapid change from a rural to an urban society. The student body reflected this trend in pushing for less emphasis on and association with agriculture, and for more opportunities that would be characteristic of a college of arts and sciences.

The decade following Goodell's presidency was also one of growth and change. The physical facilities on campus were improved and expanded. The student body became more cosmopolitan and the requirement of manual labor was dropped. The administrative staff was restructured and enlarged. By 1916 the faculty numbered over 70, some 275 courses were offered, and the student population had more than doubled to nearly 600 undergraduate and 50 graduate enrollees. The faculty itself was organized into 23 departmental units with the latter grouped in 5 divisions. These were science, horticulture and landscape gardening, agriculture, humanities, and rural social science. Rural social science, which was new to Massachusetts Agricultural College, included agricultural economics, education, and rural sociology. An agricultural extension unit, which encompassed all pursuits outside of those related directly to degree programs, was also added. A number of activities already present on campus, such as the offering of short winter courses, were placed in the extension unit. A summer school was added to it in 1907 and agricultural clubs for boys and girls in Hampshire County were established in 1908. But in spite of the movement toward industrialization and urbanization in Massachusetts and American society and the pressures that arose from it, the College remained focused almost exclusively on agriculture. The introduction of wider educational possibilities in liberal arts and sciences was still some years away.

It is not surprising that World War I had a profound impact on Massachusetts Agricultural College. The school year was shortened to permit students more time to work on farms that were producing food for the war effort. Student enrollments plummeted as young men entered the armed forces. The size of the faculty declined for the same reason. And a Reserve Officers Training Corps unit was established on campus at the end of 1917.

The College recovered quickly after the war, but the seeds for change had been planted. World War I had brought women into industry, agriculture, and the military in significant numbers. This, in turn, led to a considerable advancement in the recognition of women's rights, including the right, if desired, to a college education. Although women had been admitted to Massachusetts Agricultural College since 1892, their numbers as of the fall of 1917 added up to a grand total of 30. But by 1920, this number would double, and there would be a dormitory on campus that could house up to 100 women. In addition, special programs would be introduced and designed specifically for them.

But the most significant change in store for the College was the profound transformation of its relationship to the State of Massachusetts. In legislative sessions of 1918 and 1919, the College's charter was terminated, and the College was merged with the state bureaucracy under the direction of the commissioner of education. A new budget system was introduced that deprived the College of the financial flexibility needed to meet unusual circumstances. It was also required to return all revenues it received (from tuition and the sale of products) to the state treasury. The only funds that could be spent were those appropriated in the rigid categories defined by the legislature. Moreover, state controls over salaries, titles, and duties, among other things, were imposed. Perhaps most damaging of all, appropriations for salaries and maintenance failed to increase as needed, and requests for new buildings were, but for two exceptions, largely ignored.

The consequences of the combination of budgetary stringency and the imposition of state controls were devastating. With better-paying positions available elsewhere, faculty and staff turnover became a serious problem. Between 1918 and 1923 about half of the key personnel on campus left and had to be replaced. By 1920, departures had wiped out all social-science faculty, although, for a brief period thereafter, courses in history and government were taught by an assistant professor. But from 1922 to 1924, no courses in social science were offered. The greatest loss, however, was the resignation of president Kenyon L. Butterfield, whose outstanding leadership was to a considerable extent responsible for the College's substantial growth and development between 1906 (when he assumed the presidency) and 1916. Butterfield, citing the imposition of state controls, left to become president of Michigan State College in 1924.

Toward the end of the 1920s, the forces that were pushing to transform Massachusetts Agricultural College into a more liberal-arts-directed state college or university were gaining momentum. There were increased demands for admission by the general public, and the state's industrial centers, presumably desiring graduates who were trained for positions in industry, were pressing for the establishment of a university. Student urgings for more liberal-arts types of opportunities became more aggressive and took the form of agitating for the creation of an arts degree program. Among the students' efforts was a successful enlistment of the support of the alumni. In November of 1930 the trustees were also persuaded to join the chorus. A bill to rename the College (without any provision for redefining its educational purpose or orientation) passed the legislature and was signed by Governor Joseph B. Ely on March 26, 1931. Massachusetts Agricultural College had become Massachusetts State College.

By 1931, the student population had grown to 760, of which 210 were women. But with the primary aim of servicing agricultural needs remaining intact, there had been little alteration in the College's organization and educational programs since Butterfield's departure in 1924. The main exception was the creation of a new division of social science and the movement within that division to more general approaches in some disciplines and away from what had become the traditional focus of those disciplines on matters that related to agriculture.

In spite of the difficulties imposed by the Great Depression, more substantial changes occurred over the next eight years. As of 1933, the student population stood at 1,220. However, because there was no more room on campus in dormitories, and because there was no money for expansion, a moratorium on growth of the student population was declared for several years. Although the College had been resisting and was continuing to resist a hasty rush toward liberal arts, it still permitted movement in that direction by starting the process of establishing single departments for each of the disciplines in the social-science division. The agricultural economics courses in that division were moved into the division of agriculture, and a new Department of Economics in the division of social science was established in 1935. Initially, the Economics Department consisted of, and was headed by, Alexander E. Cance. But shortly after its creation it was expanded to three with the hiring of Phillip L. Gamble and Russell C. Larcom. Gamble became head of the Department in 1942.

By 1938 the pressures to offer a Bachelor of Arts degree could no longer be resisted and the awarding of it was approved by the trustees. At the same time, the social science division was renamed the Division of Liberal Arts. With some money becoming available from the Federal government, the number of students was permitted to rise to 1,500. A private initiative made possible the addition of two new dormitories in the early 1940s. But in spite of the expanding demands for admission by the citizens of Massachusetts, and in spite of the increasing need to upgrade and add new facilities, the state remained unwilling to provide the funding required for either purpose.

The decision to award a Bachelor of Arts degree did not quell the interest in turning Massachusetts State College into a university. Momentum in this direction began to build in 1940. Enrollments were creeping up (another moratorium on growth was imposed when the student population passed 1,700) and an increasing number of qualified students had to be denied admission. Vermont, New Hampshire, and Maine had already decided to convert their land-grant colleges into universities. The College's alumni led the transformation-into-university movement in Massachusetts. With a concerted effort, they gained the support of the president, the trustees, and the students. But as late as the summer of 1941 at the end of the legislative session of that year, the legislature would not acquiesce. Before the next legislative session could begin and permit the issue to be raised again, the country was at war, and attention was turned to other matters.

As with the World War I, the coming of World War II led to the exodus of male students and faculty from the university and into the armed forces. By 1944 student enrollments had dropped to 725, of which 600 were women. But at the war's end, with the passage of the so-called G.I. Bill that provided financial aid for higher education to all those desiring it who had served in the country's armed forces, the demand for college education all across the country became massive. Like many other colleges and universities, Massachusetts State College, with a facility that was barely adequate for 1,700 students, was ill prepared for the onslaught.

To handle the influx of students, buildings from army and navy training centers were moved to campus. The Federal Public Housing Authority erected others. The state allocated funds for still more. And, using the buildings that were already there, a temporary branch of Massachusetts State College was opened at Fort Devens northwest of Boston. The branch was intended as a two-year college whose graduates would, should they wish, continue for two more years as juniors and seniors at the College in Amherst. It remained in operation for three academic years.

During the same period, the pressure to turn Massachusetts State College into a university re-emerged. In addition to the large numbers desiring admission, the technological advances during the war, among other factors, led to a demand for programs in engineering, business administration, and teacher training. Political support for the change was increasing, and student activism that included the lobbying of state politicians was considerable. On May 6, 1947, Governor Robert A. Bradford signed the bill, passed by the legislature, which converted the College into the University of Massachusetts.

In 1947, the University of Massachusetts was a university in name only. Much needed to be done to transform it into an institution that would be worthy of its new identity. To achieve that goal, a more appropriate organizational structure, considerably enlarged and improved physical facilities, an expanded and extended curriculum, and a substantial increase in the number of faculty (among other things) were all necessary. By the early 1960s, considerable progress had been made. The legislature had given the University complete authority over appointments and personnel actions,[2] and sufficient flexibility over the salaries of new appointees to enable it to compete successfully for accomplished scholars. (University revenues from tuition, however, still had to be turned over to the state.) The financial and business operations of the University had been reorganized and largely freed from state supervision, and the position of provost had been created. The liberal arts and sciences had been combined into one school (the College of Arts and Sciences), and agriculture and horticulture into another (the Stockbridge

---

2. The award of tenure could now be based on an evaluation of a faculty member's performance. Previously, faculty members, as part of the state bureaucracy, were classified as civil servants and, as such, were automatically granted tenure upon completion of the requisite number of years in their positions.

School of Agriculture). Separate schools of home economics, engineering, business administration (as distinct from the Department of Economics, which had, in part, been teaching business courses up until then), education, nursing, and physical education had been established. With the state finally cooperating in the provision of funds, building activity had been extensive. The student body had grown to 6,500 and the size of the faculty to 580.

The years 1945–1970 have been referred to as the golden age for American universities.[3] That twenty-five-year span saw a continual and more or less uninterrupted expansion fueled by both massive demand for student admissions and the national research effort to catch up to Soviet space exploration after the successful launch of their Sputnik I in 1957. By the end of the period, enrollments at the Amherst campus of the University of Massachusetts had soared to almost 18,000 and faculty size had almost doubled to about 1,000. At long last, the University seemed to have joined the community of full-fledged, land-grant, public universities scattered across the country. Along with research service for the general public and nondegree instruction, it offered a considerable number of strong graduate-degree programs and was engaged in a variety of significant research activities—both of which were built on a large undergraduate base. A Boston campus for commuting students who could not afford a residential college education was approved by the state legislature in 1964 and opened fifteen months later in September of 1965. Also in 1964, a decision to establish a medical school in Worcester was made by the University's trustees. Toward the end of the decade, the University trustees introduced an improved organizational structure in which each campus would

3. R.M. Freeland, *Academia's Golden Age: Universities in Massachusetts, 1945–1970* (New York: Oxford University Press, 1992), p. 70.

be autonomous and headed by a chancellor. A president would oversee the entire system, setting budget priorities, determining general policies, engaging in overall planning, and representing the University to the state and other constituencies. An office for the president was opened near the state house (some distance from the Boston campus) in the fall of 1970.

It was during the 1960s that the University moved to establish the major graduate-program and research credentials already described. This was part of president John W. Lederle's attempt to raise the prestige of the University of Massachusetts to a level comparable to that of the best private institutions. Thirty-four new PhD programs were added, the hiring of new faculty focused on research-oriented scholars, and the older faculty who, over the years, had mostly taught classes and eschewed research, were encouraged to engage in research projects.

Also during the 1960s, two political constituencies arose that attempted to impose restraint on the University's expansion program. First, the growth of the University of Massachusetts was seen as a threat by the private colleges and universities in the state—especially those who traditionally drew large numbers of their students from the pool of Massachusetts's high school students. These institutions banded together to try, by restricting the ability of the University of Massachusetts to expand, to prevent it from drawing too heavily on that pool. Secondly, the state colleges that were independent of the University of Massachusetts and a newly created network of community colleges all competed with the University for limited financial support from the legislature. In spite of these efforts, University expansion and development in the 1960s was robust. Indeed, by 1970 a consolidation of academic programs generally encountered at the traditional university level, along with a faculty of considerable quality to match, had been achieved, and a more secure foundation had been laid for progress and for managing the difficulties that lay ahead.

Those difficulties were not long in coming. For example, since the mid 1970s, serious budget problems have re-emerged. University budget requests have been frequently and significantly cut by the legislature. There have been freezes on hiring and salary increases, budgetary recisions on funds previously allocated by the state, deferred maintenance of physical facilities, early retirement programs, and general attrition as faculty found more congenial financial and academic environments elsewhere. Between 1987 and 2004, the number of tenured faculty on the Amherst campus declined by 243 or 25 percent, and the number of faculty in tenure tracks declined by 37 or 15 percent.[4]

There have been other interferences as well. For example, on the tenth of June in 1980, without any public discussion or review by interested parties, the legislature passed and Governor Edward J. King subsequently signed a budget bill that contained a section reorganizing the entire public higher education system in Massachusetts under a Board of Regents. In an editorial the next day, the Boston Globe reacted, in part, as follows: The reorganization "... involved deals and 'understandings' and pressures that had very little to do with the quality of this state's public higher-education system ..." and "It will be no surprise if the ... reorganization ... does not work; it will be a miracle if it does." In July of 1991, Governor William F. Weld signed legislation that incorporated the University of Lowell and Southeastern Massachusetts University (at Dartmouth) into the now five-campus University of Massachusetts system. And the Board of Regents was replaced with a less powerful Higher

---

4. From a "Fact Sheet" prepared by the Office of Institutional Research, University of Massachusetts at Amherst.

Education Coordinating Council to oversee the performance of
public higher education in Massachusetts.

A plausible explanation of why the University of Massachusetts
has been so severely buffeted on budgetary and other matters
throughout its history by the winds of state politics has been provided by Ronald Story:[5] The problem, he says, is partly one of
ideology.

> The rhetoric of democracy and opportunity, of joined hands and
> helping hands, has underlain every phase of University prosperity....
> And the reality has mostly matched the rhetoric. In 1910, two-thirds
> of the students were from farming or wage-earning families; in 1930,
> 80 percent worked to pay their bills, and in 1990 three-quarters still
> did. The citizenry, however,... [has lacked] faith in government, in
> opportunity, in generosity of spirit, in democratic initiative—even,
> it sometimes seems, in the possibility of a culture held in common
> or, indeed, in the efficacy of informed reason itself. In such circum-
> stances an institution predicated on public purpose, democratic
> aspiration, and the life of the mind is bound to have rough sledding.
> The results are evident not only at the University of Massachusetts
> but at universities, public and private, throughout the country

However, there are differences between other states like California
and Michigan, say, and Massachusetts. One of them is that the
public universities in those states have been providing for over
100 years large-scale, high-quality education that has benefited
tens of thousands of California and Michigan opinion makers.
Because legislators and the public generally give money only for

5. "The Ordeal of the Public Sector: The University of Massachusetts," *Five Colleges: Five Histories*, R. Story, ed. (Amherst: Five Colleges Inc., Historic Deerfield Inc., 1992), pp. 68–69.

undergraduate education and not for research, a massive political constituency sympathetic to public education has been available to support public universities in those states for a long time. Moreover, in many midwestern states, public universities have provided considerable service and research support to their relatively large agricultural communities, which have, in turn, significantly added to those universities' political constituencies. Those states generally do not have large numbers of private institutions competing for students with the public universities. However, the University of Massachusetts has only begun to establish its own constituency relatively recently—toward the end of the 1960s. The agricultural community in Massachusetts is comparatively quite small and, despite the help it has received from the University, is not large enough to have the same political effect as agricultural communities in the Midwest. Furthermore, there are many private and public colleges and universities in Massachusetts which, because they compete with the University for students, would prefer to keep the University of Massachusetts small. Thus the University's political constituency has not yet become big enough and strong enough to overcome public apathy and pressures from the private institutions and the state and community colleges, and to insulate significantly the University from the vagaries of state politics.

Regardless, for whatever reason or reasons, as the foregoing brief historical survey shows, with the exception of a period of approximately twenty-eight years after World War II and in spite of several earlier intervals of growth, the state of Massachusetts has not been especially kind to the institution made up of the University and its precursors. It has meddled with the institution's organizational structure in a number of ways and sometimes subjected it to ill-thought-out political whims. Only reluctantly and after many protracted efforts did it give up state control over such things as faculty appointments, salaries, and duties. The financial support it has provided over the years has been, at best, lukewarm, and often downright stingy. Such miserliness has frequently caused episodes of considerable retrenchment and deterioration of the quality of the institution and its faculty, and it also has prevented the institution from reaching its full potential. And after each retrenchment episode, a costly process of rebuilding had to be undertaken.

Still, the tampering notwithstanding, the one thing that the state has *not* done is to interfere significantly in the intellectual activity in which the University, and the colleges before it, have engaged. In the grand tradition of Massachusetts liberalism, faculty have been mostly free to pursue their intellectual endeavors in the absence of any censorship pressure by the state. Specifically, in spite of the considerable fear across the United States of Communism and the Soviet Union that was exacerbated by the McCarthy era investigations of Communists in the U.S. government and which lasted into the 1970s and early 1980s, and in spite of the intellectual ties to Marxism that were clearly present, there was never a hint of disapproval or condemnation directed toward the (radical) political economy program or the (radical) faculty of the Economics Department on the Amherst campus of the University of Massachusetts.[6] This has certainly not been true elsewhere. For example, in 1978 the Department of Government on the College Park campus of the University of Maryland enthusiastically endorsed the hiring of

---

6. Another example of this absence of state interference in the University's scholarly affairs during the fear-of-Communism period was the acquisition of W.E.B. DuBois's papers for the University's library. DuBois was among the most prominent and influential black scholars of the twentieth century. But he was also an acknowledged Communist who, by the time of his death in 1963, had surrendered his American citizenship to become a citizen of Ghana. Negotiations for DuBois's papers began at the end of 1971 with DuBois's wife, and the papers came to the library in 1973. Twenty-one years later in October of 1994, the University's Board of Trustees voted to name the University's main library in DuBois's honor.

Bertell Ollman, a distinguished Marxist political scientist from another university, as Department chairman. This appointment was approved by the University's provost and chancellor. But the state's acting governor and several state legislators threatened to cut the University's budget if the appointment were confirmed. The president of the University caved in to the pressure and vetoed the appointment.[7]

7. "The Case of the Marxist Professor," *The News York Times*, July 28, 1978: A22.

Chapter 3

The Civil Rights and Vietnam War Protest Movements

Economics,[1] as has been said, is an academic discipline whose cultivation is informed by a wide range of socially relevant questions. Its practitioners have imaginatively addressed the problems and policies that stem from concern for human betterment—both in the small, as with investigations of individual and market behaviors, and on the broader canvas of economy-wide considerations of employment, price stability, and growth. These same concerns have come to expression in the Economics Department on the Amherst campus of the University of Massachusetts in terms of a diversity of analytical paradigms, each with its own emphasis and social significance, which have contributed a catholicity of scholarship to the University community.

Of course, the parentage of the diversity that is here in view can be understood only against the background of social, political, and cultural developments in the United States at large. For this reason it is necessary to delve into some aspects of U.S. history, particularly those pertaining to certain movements of protest and agitation for social, economic, and political change. These movements, it turns

1. Except as otherwise noted, this chapter is dependent on "Vietnam War" from v. 23 of *Colliers Encyclopedia* (1997) and the following entries from the 1999 edition of *Encyclopedia Americana*: "Civil Disobedience" and "Civil Rights Movement" (v. 6), "Students for a Democratic Society" (v. 25), and "Vietnam War" (v. 28).

out, had important implications for conditions and developments at the University of Massachusetts at Amherst. As will be seen in subsequent chapters, their influence extended in various ways to the staffing and nature of academic programs in its Economics Department. Present considerations begin with what became a most prominent instance in the long struggle against the general and extensive discriminatory practices of white America directed toward the country's black community.

Efforts by various groups and individuals to end racial discrimination and secure equality in a variety of forms for American blacks go back a long way. Although black people were in principle as free and equal as whites as a consequence of the Thirteenth, Fourteenth, and Fifteenth Amendments to the U.S. Constitution adopted between 1865 and 1870, in actual fact that precept did not apply or was ignored in many situations. Laws were enacted and practices developed that effectively segregated blacks from white communities. Among other things, they were denied voting rights, equal access to public accommodations, equal rights in courts, and equality of opportunity in education, housing, and securing work. Over time, a few organizations, such as the National Association for the Advancement of Colored People and the Urban League, were formed to address and redress such incursions on black freedom and equality. In the early years, these groups were nonconfrontational and did not openly challenge the white power structure. They devoted their attention to legal action, to boycotts against businesses that would not employ black people, and to helping the black community adjust to various living conditions in a variety of places. However, by the 1940s, the feeling became widespread that such efforts, by themselves, would not end racial discrimination and that it would be necessary to confront the white community in a more direct way. The Congress of Racial Equality, organized in 1942, began to stage sit-ins in restaurants and stand-ins in swimming pools where blacks were not permitted to go. What is commonly referred to as the civil rights movement is the considerably more extensive and intensified activity during the 1950s and 1960s that was pointed toward breaking the chains of segregation and bringing equal voting, educational, housing, and economic opportunities to black people.

The tide began to turn in May of 1954 when the Supreme Court ruled that compulsory segregation in public schools was in violation of the equal protection to all citizens guaranteed by the Fourteenth Amendment. In the following year it ordered that integration of those schools be carried out "with all deliberate speed." However, given the numerous road blocks already placed in the path of desegregation, all deliberate speed turned out to be painfully slow. Integration of public schools and universities required considerable litigation, involved substantial violence, and often necessitated the use of federal marshals and occasionally federal troops.

The civil rights movement itself was galvanized in December of 1955 when, in Montgomery, Alabama, Rosa Parks, a black seamstress, was arrested for not giving up her seat on a bus to a white passenger. That arrest was immediately followed by a successful boycott, under the leadership of The Reverend Martin Luther King, of the bus company on whose bus the arrest was made. The success of that boycott led to the creation of the Southern Christian Leadership Conference, also led by King, and to a mass movement in which King played a major role, to breach the barriers of segregation and racial discrimination everywhere and especially in the South.

King's tactics were to create a crisis through nonviolent civil disobedience that would directly confront the individuals and institutions who would stand in the way. His methods were similar to those of Mahatma Gandhi who had, some years earlier, been involved in the struggle for the independence of India from Great Britain. King understood that the white community respected established law and the individual rights it protected. His aim was to appeal to white citizens' conscience and sense of justice, and to convince them of the unfairness perpetrated by racial discrimination against the black community without alienating them from his cause. In this he was quite successful. With the aid of the Student Nonviolent Coordinating Committee, which he helped to organize, young whites journeyed from northern states to the South to join in sit-ins at segregated lunch counters, pray-ins at segregated churches, wade-ins at segregated beaches, marches, demonstrations, and other forms of protest. They and their southern compatriots, black and some white, endured verbal and physical abuse without yielding to the desire to retaliate in any form. Their deportment and the publicity that came with it generated widespread sympathy and expanded their numbers. Other student groups, such as the Students for a Democratic Society formed in Chicago in 1960, entered the fray. Gradually, the American public became convinced of the moral imperative and legal legitimacy of efforts to end the racial discrimination against black persons. Large demonstrations protesting that discrimination were organized around the country. In August of 1963, more than 250,000 people from all over the United States, white and black, gathered in front of the Lincoln memorial in Washington, D.C., to hear King passionately intone, "I have a dream that... one day... [in America, individuals] will not be judged by the color of their skin but by the content of their character."

Congress responded to the building pressure. A southern filibuster was broken and the Civil Rights Act of 1964 was passed making racial discrimination in the use of most public facilities illegal. Shortly thereafter, the Voting Rights Act of 1965 eliminated certain voter tests and poll taxes, and empowered federal examiners to register voters in specific cases. Black America seemed to have achieved a good measure of the equality it sought.

But there was still a long way to go, and at this point, violence and disarray began to overtake the civil rights movement. Riots occurred in black sections of Los Angeles, Newark, Detroit, and elsewhere. Stokely Carmichael, who had become chairman of the Student Nonviolent Coordinating Committee, advocated retaliatory violence as a legitimate means to end racial discrimination, and a considerable number of blacks and whites responded by withdrawing from the organization. As the Student Nonviolent Coordinating Committee and other black groups assumed a more militant posture, many black communities began to turn inward, emphasizing self-determination and self-respect. Martin Luther King was assassinated on April 4, 1968. The drive to eliminate racial discrimination continued in fragmented form, its intensity significantly diminished by disunity. And there was now a new moral crisis that demanded the attention of many of those who had so fervently pushed for black civil rights—the Vietnam War.

The origins of the Vietnam War reside in events that took place some years earlier. At the end of World War II, the defeated Japanese left Indochina and were immediately replaced by the French who returned as colonial administrators. However, by 1946 France found itself in war against Communist insurgents who had proclaimed an independent Vietnamese government the previous year. Maintaining its control over the region, the French granted nominal sovereignty to Vietnam, Cambodia, and Laos. Nevertheless the war continued, with considerable support for France coming from the United States. But in spite of U.S. help, the French did not do well. The agreement that ended the war in 1954 after France had suffered many military defeats provided that the French would abandon the area. With respect to Vietnam, it was agreed, among other things, that the country would be temporarily divided into North and South, and that elections would be held in two years to select a government for a unified nation. After France withdrew her troops, the Communists quickly consolidated their hold on North Vietnam and the former French-controlled, anti-Communist government in South Vietnam was supported by the United States. Official U.S. policy for the region at that time was based on the so-called domino theory that held that, were South Vietnam to fall to the Communists, the remaining countries in the area would, like a collapsing sequence of standing dominos, succumb as well. Fearing that the Communists would win, the South Vietnamese government, with the backing of the United States, blocked the national election that was to be held in 1956. The possibility of reuniting the country by election had now been eliminated, and the Communist insurgents in the South who had previously fought the French became active again. Supported by the North, terrorist actions in the South were begun in 1957 and this is often said to be the start of the Vietnam War.

By 1964, regular army units from North Vietnam had joined the Communist insurgents in the South. In an attempt to build a strong South Vietnamese army, the United States had already provided money and military equipment, ammunitions, and advisers. But the result was a corrupt and generally inept fighting force and, as a result, large portions of South Vietnam had fallen under Communist control. On two separate days in August of 1964, attacks by North Vietnam on American ships patrolling in the Gulf of Tonkin prompted President Lyndon B. Johnson to order the bombing of North Vietnamese naval installations. Johnson used the Gulf of Tonkin assaults to secure passage of a Congressional resolution giving him the authority to repel attacks on U.S. forces and prevent further aggression in Vietnam. Although Johnson took this resolution as the legal basis for an undeclared war against the North, some question arose about whether the administration had misrepresented what had happened in the Gulf, and the resolution was repealed in 1970.

The American commitment of troops to the Vietnam War rose substantially after the Tonkin Gulf incidents and the Congressional resolution of 1964. Regular bombing of North Vietnam by U.S. aircraft began in 1965. The guerrilla nature of the war changed when the North and southern Communist insurgents began to challenge South Vietnamese and American troops in relatively large, open battles. Hostilities spread to Cambodia and Laos in 1970 as the United States attempted to interrupt the flow of North Vietnamese supplies of men and ammunition through those countries to operations in the South. Militarily, the war turned into a stalemate with both sides experiencing defeats and victories. In one of the more significant events, the North Vietnamese and southern insurgents' Tet offensive in January of 1968, although eventually defeated by U.S. and South Vietnamese forces, was a serious psychological setback for Americans. A peace accord was signed in Paris in January of 1973 that provided for a cease-fire, a temporary continuation of the division between North and South, the withdrawal of all U.S. military forces, and an end to the American bombing of North Vietnam. But after the departure of U.S. troops, the fighting between North and South continued until the Southern capital city, Saigon, fell to the Communists in April of 1975.

The cost of the war was immense. Almost 58,000 Americans lost their lives and over 300,000 were wounded. The South Vietnamese military casualties numbered approximately 220,000 and 500,000, respectively. The Communists' losses were estimated at 440,000 and the number of wounded is unknown. These figures do not include the hundreds of thousands of civilian casualties. The economies of both North and South were shattered, and about half of South Vietnam's population had become refugees in their own country. The official dollar cost of the war to the United States amounted to $165 billion.

The effect of the Vietnam War on American society was profound. Many clergy, educators, and businessmen had disapproved of the U.S. involvement early on. With the media regularly and vividly bringing the enormous devastation and carnage from the war into American homes, with the seemingly endless stream of dead soldiers returning to the country for burial, and with the psychological impact of the Tet offensive, the unpopularity of the war spread. Much of the opposition to it coalesced behind the candidacy of Senator Eugene J. McCarthy in his bid for the Democratic presidential nomination in 1968. Although McCarthy was unable to secure the nomination for himself, he was so successful that President Johnson felt his leadership had been repudiated and decided not to run for a second term of office. At that time, a majority of the American public still did not favor disengagement from Vietnam; but by 1971, it did.

Of all American groups opposing U.S. involvement in Vietnam, none was more passionate than the country's youth. Many had participated in or witnessed the struggle for black civil rights and, as a result of the strong hostility that struggle had aroused, had begun to lose faith in America's compassion for justice and its capitalist economic system. And they were now faced with massive death and destruction that in their view could not be vindicated in any rational or moral way. In their minds, American society had to be changed. The impact on their emerging radicalization and polarization was considerable and their opposition to the war intense. The young were a major driving force in McCarthy's presidential bid. Ten thousand of them demonstrated their opposition to the war (and provoked a violent police response) at the Democratic presidential-nominating convention in Chicago in August of 1968 and generally dominated the war-protest movement. Groups like the Students for a Democratic Society changed their focus from the civil rights to antiwar action. They encouraged resistance to the armed forces draft that was in place at the time, and they organized numerous demonstrations. In the spring of 1970, largely in response to the widening of the Vietnam War to Cambodia, almost all college campuses experienced disruption from student antiwar activity. Four students were fatally shot and ten wounded by the Ohio National Guard unit that had been deployed to quell a demonstration at Kent State University. Two more were killed and twelve wounded by police ten days later at Jackson State College in Mississippi. Perhaps because it was so dramatic and the violence it produced so horrifying, this sort of opposition drew the greatest attention and, in addition to the factors cited above, played a significant role in shifting American public opinion against the war. Not surprisingly, such protest activity against the war continued until the signing of the peace accord in 1973.

Although, as noted in Chapter 2, student confrontational activity at the University of Massachusetts dates to the first class that entered Massachusetts Agricultural College in 1867, collective student action on the Amherst campus as of the mid 1960s, including civil rights and Vietnam War protests, lagged well behind those at other colleges and universities, both in frequency and in intensity.[2] By the start of 1967, restrictions on deportment that had severely limited student behavior in general had been dismantled on many

2. This and the next five paragraphs are heavily dependent on T. J. Martin, "Student Movements at the University of Massachusetts Amherst in the Late Nineteen Sixties," University of Massachusetts Honors Project, February, 2004.

campuses across the country in response to student demonstrations against them. The rioting in black inner cities and the repudiation of nonviolent action by some black civil rights leaders mentioned earlier had begun, as a matter of course, to impact the protest activities and demands of black students. Confrontational action in opposition to the Vietnam War, to campus recruitment by companies supplying materiel for the war effort, to the military draft, and to the presence of Reserve Officer Training Corps units on campuses had become commonplace. But at the University of Massachusetts, things were still relatively quiet.

The year 1967 saw the beginnings of significant collective student action on the Amherst campus. The main focus of attention was an effort to eliminate the deportment restrictions imposed on students by the administration. There were many discussions among various groups at all levels and some progress was made. But student activities in this regard did not cause any serious disruptions in the operations of the University.

The first significant student demonstration at the University of Massachusetts at Amherst during this period occurred in February, 1968. It started as a protest against Dow Chemical Company, the primary producer of napalm for use by the United States in the Vietnam War effort, which was attempting to recruit new employees on campus. Very quickly, however, the focus of the protest shifted to the restrictions still in place on student deportment. The students wanted greater input over policies and procedures that affected them directly. They demanded a dialogue with the administration on such matters and, in particular, a more open housing policy. But there was still moderation and little militancy. The students desired change within the system. They were not yet prone to aggressive and highly confrontational tactics. After the demonstration, which succeeded in venting and publicizing their demands, student activity continued to push in three main areas: (1) dropping academic credit for taking Reserve Officer Training Corps courses, (2) freedom and autonomy in choosing housing, and (3) on various racial issues, such as the admission of more black students, the hiring of more black professors, a greater emphasis on black culture, and a building that would be a center for black people on campus.

As black confrontational tactics and forceful opposition to the Vietnam War heated up elsewhere, militancy finally spilled over onto the Amherst branch of the University of Massachusetts. In February of 1969, thirty-three students protesting once again the presence of Dow Chemical recruiters on campus were arrested by State police for refusing to leave the Whitmore administration building. The following March, a small group of students prevented Senator Strom Thurmond, one of the main symbols of resistance to the redressing of racial discrimination, from speaking at the University.[3] Although large numbers of people were unhappy with the use of the state police and the abrogation of free speech, these events paled in significance when compared to the violence at other colleges and universities around the country. There were still protest actions at the University of Massachusetts at Amherst that remained nonviolent and peaceful, including a large antiwar demonstration in October of that year. It is also interesting that during 1969, campus-housing policies were considerably liberalized by the board of trustees, and the faculty senate voted to discontinue academic credit for all Reserve Officer Training Corps courses that were not taught by official University personnel—thus meeting, at least in part, two of the students' major demands.

As was true at campuses around the country, the number, size, and intensity of student protests at the University of Massachusetts at Amherst exploded during the Spring of 1970 with the expansion

3. In addition to heckling, at one point a student took the microphone from him.

of the Vietnam War into Cambodia. There was heated opposition to dormitory rent increases triggered by state cuts to the University's budget, and demands for a greater role in certain University decision processes and for faster administrative action on the creation of a Black Studies department (which the administration had already agreed in 1968 to establish). Vice President Hubert H. Humphrey was "tried" on campus for not attempting to prevent the police brutality toward Vietnam-War protesters at the 1968 Democratic convention in Chicago and, like Senator Thurmond before him, was prevented from speaking to a University audience. There was a demonstration against recruitment by another company, Honeywell, which had supplied materiel to the Vietnam War effort. And large numbers of students participated in the local University contribution to a massive nationwide, multicampus strike against the War. The University of Massachusetts at Amherst had caught up to the rest of the country insofar as the frequency and intensity of student protest activity were concerned. However, in all of these later protests on the Amherst campus, both faculty and administrators became deeply involved in channeling student anger into peaceful outlets and in working out compromises.[4] No one, not even the students, wanted a repeat of the extreme confrontations and arrests of 1969.

4. For example, in response to a physical assault on black students by members of a white fraternity at the end of February in 1970, blacks took over Mills dormitory, the first floor of which had come to be known as a place for them to meet. The white students living there were forced out. Shortly thereafter, the chancellor of the University, Oswald Tippo, while asking the governor to delay state intervention and give the University time to work something out, convinced the black students that the state would not tolerate the takeover and that they had to leave. Upon their departure, the white residents were found another place to live and the administration agreed, in jumping ahead of preliminary discussions on the matter, to turn Mills dormitory into a black cultural center. See *Oswald Tippo and the Early Promise of the University of Massachusetts*, compiled and edited by I. Seidman (Amherst: Friends of the University of Massachusetts Library, 2002), pp. 70–72.

It is clear that student civil rights and Vietnam War protests on the Amherst campus of the University of Massachusetts up to 1970 did not achieve the level of militancy and violence at other colleges and universities across the United States. Three reasons have been given for this moderation:

> First, the culture [of protest action] at ... [the University of Massachusetts at Amherst] remained years behind other schools, and it was only in the late [nineteen-]sixties that the University began to experience large-scale demonstrations. Although activity at the University echoed the changes that were occurring on other college campuses, ... [University of Massachusetts] students were never [in] the vanguard of [that] change [and were therefore less prone to militancy and violence]. Secondly, students never faced a reactionary or repressive administration of the sort that often turned many students toward radicalism [and extreme militancy] at other campuses. Lastly, the faculty were supportive of student concerns and rights, and gave student activists a guiding presence to help their movements reach constructive and positive ends.[5]

At any rate, by 1970 student protest activity had come abreast with that on other campuses around the country and remained apace well into the next decade. The faculty and administration continued their efforts to keep matters under control by supporting and accommodating student demands as far as they could.

The environment on the Amherst campus between 1969 and 1973, from the perspective of a faculty member involved in the

---

5. T. J. Martin, "Student Movements at the University of Massachusetts Amherst in the Late Nineteen Sixties," University of Massachusetts Honors Project, February, 2004, Abstract.

protest movement, has been described by Michael H. Best, then in the University's Economics Department, as follows:

> It is hard to capture the extraordinary mood and character of the times at the University of Massachusetts. It was tumultuous and exciting. The place was hopping like never before and, I would guess, never again. It was a great place to be in those years. I do not think any other campus in the Northeast was as active and it drew the best and the brightest in the anti-war movement. It was the only place that could hold a Union of Radical Political Economy conference and fill the largest lecture hall on campus. This is what made it attractive to me, someone from the woods of Montana. It was an easy entry into the world of education in places I had never dreamed of attending or experiencing. Moreover, it was as much an intellectual movement as a political movement. There was an intellectual excitement which cut across departments and campuses. We were reading, writing, lecturing, and seminaring in an atmosphere of intellectual vitality and openness that is not often present.[6]

Of course, not everyone viewed the protest movement so positively.

6. Edited from e-mail correspondence dated March 13, 2008. Reproduced with permission.

Chapter 4

The American Economics Profession

In addition to the social, political, and cultural environment present in the United States during the 1960s and 1970s, developments within the economics profession itself also played a significant role in bringing together a major group of radical economists in the Economics Department of the University of Massachusetts at Amherst. The history of that profession and the relevant developments are considered in this chapter.

The American economics social-scientific community, or what will be referred to as the (American) economics profession, may be thought of as emerging with the creation of the American Economic Association at a meeting in Saratoga, New York in 1885.[1] Its leadership, including its first secretary, Richard T. Ely, believed that research in economics should be relevant to real world problems and that the new association should play a role in the dissemination of well-founded economic ideas and the shaping of economic public policy. But within the first thirty years of its existence, controversy over advocacy versus objectivity had led to a push toward more objective or scientific methods than were

---

1. The following paragraphs on the general history of the economics profession are derived from Michael A. Bernstein, *A Perilous Progress: Economists and Public Purpose in Twentieth-Century America* (Princeton: Princeton University Press, 2001).

previously employed. In pursuit of that goal, theory became of paramount importance; its relevance to reality and policy less so. Indeed, the engagement of policy was thought to open the door to pernicious subjective values and propaganda justifications. Reflecting these sentiments, a small number of select economists developed standards for publication in the Association's new journal, *The American Economic Review*, the first issue of which came out in 1911. The standards created were not only undemocratic in their determination but they also tended to be exclusionary in that they reflected only the views of their creators. Nevertheless, it was in this way that economists were trying to demonstrate their professionalism and scientism, and thereby gain public respect. However, by and large, that respect was not forthcoming, and the profession remained ignored by the general public and also by the government in its making of economic policy.

World War I temporarily reduced the profession's insularity as large numbers of economists moved into a variety of government agencies to deal with real-world economic matters. But with the demobilization after the war and the shrinkage of government that followed, they left the public sector almost as quickly as they had entered, and the profession's public reputation more or less returned to what it had been before the war. Economists looked anew for a place to demonstrate the usefulness and significance of their skills. The creation of the Brookings Institution and the National Bureau of Economic Research were two venues that served this purpose. And the statistical projects enthusiastically and energetically pursued by Herbert C. Hoover as secretary of commerce provided an entree into the government bureaucracy. However, apart from these exceptions, which certainly did have a positive impact on the profession's reputation at the time, the primary emphasis remained on the theoretical with little regard to real problems and policy. Focused in

this way, it is not surprising that, with Hoover still looking to economists for advice during his presidency, the economics profession
fell flat on its face. As M.A. Bernstein put it:

> ...it was a cruel irony that Hoover was so ill served by the very
> experts whom he had cultivated with such zeal. No economist
> warned him of the coming of the Great Depression a half year after
> his inauguration as president; only a few provided him with com-
> pelling and practical ideas to attempt a resolution of the crisis once
> it took hold. Hoover experienced the utter collapse of his political
> fortunes because of the impact of the very kind of national disaster
> he had looked to a professional economics to prevent.[2]

Occupying themselves mostly with arcane economic theories and
economic minutiae while the economy was teetering on the edge of
a cliff and then falling off, economists generally had little of significance to say about the catastrophe. As might be expected, in terms
of the public respect it craved, the economics profession found itself
back in the cellar where it had begun. No one paid any attention to
it or its pronouncements.

But the profession did take note of what had happened to its
reputation. Inspired by the work of John Maynard Keynes, it began
to focus attention on the macrotheoretic causes of and remedies
for the Great Depression, including examination of such possibilities as the savings paradox,[3] the liquidity trap,[4] and less-than-full-
employment macroeconomic equilibrium.[5] It dropped its neglect

2. Ibid., p. 69.
3. With everyone trying to save more, they may actually wind up saving less.
4. An interest rate so low and the desire for liquidity so widespread that lenders become unwilling to loan funds for investment and other purposes.
5. A circumstance in which the economy settles down and does not move from a level of production associated with high unemployment.

of economic-policy engagement and the American Economic Association began to encourage its membership to undertake government work. As the decade of the 1930s approached its end, more and more did precisely that. At the behest of the federal government, economists developed a system of national income accounting to measure and compare states of the economy, and became involved in the planning and mobilization for and the conduct of World War II. With respect to the latter, what had now become full-blown neoclassical economic theory was employed to resolve scarcity, distribution, scheduling, and sequencing problems as they arose in relation to defense procurement, production, management, and other war-related matters. These efforts were very successful and visible, and the economics profession's reputation rose accordingly. Such was its status at the end of the war that the profession's expertise was institutionalized within the Executive Office of the U.S. President in the creation of the Council of Economic Advisers in 1946.

With the advent of economic prosperity after the surrenders of Germany and Japan and the onset of the cold war, the opportunities for economists to display and apply their expertise to real problems did not, as they did after World War I, disappear. Among other things, economists created large-scale econometric models (applications of Keynesian theory and its extensions) for making macroeconomic policy recommendations, they helped with difficult government budgetary issues, and their theory of games found important use in the strategic planning for the defense of the United States against the Soviet Union. They also developed rationales and means of implementation for the proposition that, when markets did not function properly, they could and should be fixed by government intervention. What was deemed to be proper and what was taken to be the end toward which any fix was directed were determined by given social values that pointed toward general well-being. However, as public regard grew, economic analyses became ever more abstract and abstruse in spite of the effort to tie them into real-world problems and government policy. Because the social values involved were imposed from outside, the analyses themselves, in the minds of many of the economists who were engaged in their development and promulgation, were purportedly value free. Indeed, it was this type of analytical construction, with its emphasis on objective science and technical advance, that was thought to have brought the profession its considerable success and prestige. When the Soviets launched Sputnik I in October of 1957 and funding for the National Science Foundation (created in May of 1950) was substantially increased as part of America's effort to catch up to the Soviet Union in the race to outer space, almost half of the research funds earmarked for the social sciences went to economists. Funding from other government agencies and private foundations kept apace.

However, there was a dark underside to these achievements. In the climate created in part by the postwar fear of Communism that reached its peak during the McCarthy era investigations of 1950–1954 and beyond, the economics profession found itself suppressing the free cultivation of ideas. Not only did government secrets have to be kept for national security purposes, but economic analyses from socialist, Marxian, or radical perspectives were generally said to be wrong or well below professional standards. The latter conclusion made it easy to refuse to publish such work in the profession's leading journals and to deny their promulgators access to tenured faculty positions. However, notwithstanding the belief that economic science was value free, the ever-present tension between social science and policy, between objectivity and ideology, between intellectual conviction and political expediency remained, and the distinction between the scholarly and the political continued to blur. Moreover, as previously suggested, the profession now automatically accepted economic policy goals, and scientific economic analyses were geared toward their justification and achievement. Standards were based on neoclassical theory and associated statistical procedures, because those were thought to be the basis on which economists had achieved their scientific success and respectability. Other approaches, not only Marxian or radical, were considered to be erroneous and expelled to the margins of the field. This attitude and the behavior it signifies only added to the intellectual exclusionary practices of the economics profession which, as described earlier, had been present almost from its inception. But it had no impact on the high esteem that the profession had achieved. For by the mid-1960s, the perception had become widespread that economic science had arrived at the point where management of the economy to ensure the simultaneous maintenance of price stability, full employment, and economic growth was possible. It was only necessary to turn matters over to economists to fine-tune the real-world economic system.

This pinnacle of respect and implied power, which no other social science has ever come close to achieving, did not last long. In no small measure that respect was due to an apparently successful economic policy to stimulate the American economy pursued by the Kennedy and Johnson administrations and inspired by the Council of Economic Advisers under the chairmanship of Walter W. Heller. At the time, a lackluster performance of business activity had left unemployment hovering just under 7 percent of the civilian labor force. It was the Council that proposed, in the form of large tax reductions, the first peacetime use of federal budget deficits to invigorate the weak economy. In early 1964, Congress enacted those cuts, and by the end of that year it was "clear" that the economy was significantly and positively responding. The fine-tuning had "worked". The economic problem had been demonstrably solved and economic science had provided the solution. That being accomplished, the Council could now turn its attention to a new policy goal: the elimination of poverty through a collection of programs, part of which came to be identified with the term *Great Society*. Congress enacted those programs during the first two years of Johnson's full term in office.

Accompanying the profession's climb up the ladder of repute and success was a determination to standardize the content of undergraduate and graduate education. Training in economics came to mean the understanding of and learning the ability to apply those methods that, because they were "correct," had led the profession to its pre-eminent position. Ideas and methods deemed to be antithetical to the advancement of this economic science, including those of the Marxian or radical approach, were denied a place in the curriculum. The status and success of the profession would thereby be secured for the future. However, the effort also created a strong and extensive establishment that was able to exercise tight command over what was considered to be good economics and to ensure that the standards that had been developed in that regard were rigorously enforced. Moreover, when the respect and power of the economics profession subsequently went into decline for reasons that shall be observed later, this establishment was sufficiently well-entrenched to be able to maintain its control, adapting to the new circumstances as they emerged and modifying standards accordingly.

The events that caused the economics profession to fall from grace were not entirely its own fault. The Vietnam War and President Lyndon B. Johnson's reluctance to trim the Great Society programs set off an inflationary spiral during the late 1960s that, upon being refueled by the OPEC (Organization of Petroleum Exporting Countries) oil embargo of 1973, was to last more than a decade. Confounding the economic theory that led to the successful tax cuts passed by Congress in 1964, the unemployment rate rose along with prices during the 1970s. As a result, the fine-tuning engine that drove economists to the height of public respect and power in the 1960s was discredited. The Great Society programs and the large government bureaucracy needed to implement them, claimed by some to be the cause of the unemployment difficulties due to the imbalances they introduced, came under attack. In this environment, the economics profession lost its moorings and became unsure and confused. Out of the morass, some economists, known as supply-siders, openly eschewed the mantle of science and enlisted in the service of partisan politics on the right. They advocated significant cuts in tax rates in the belief that the increase in economic activity thereby generated would expand the tax base and government revenue. In their thinking, conservative values of private interests also replaced liberal values of communal well-being in the definition of economic policy goals: Markets were to be left to function on their own, and even if tax receipts rose, government was to be retrenched largely by eliminating programs that either interfered with business activity and profit making or were directed to helping the poor and disadvantaged. All this would enhance economic prosperity, and the benefits of that prosperity would trickle down from rich to poor.

> ...whether they intended to do so or not,...[the supply-siders provided] a rationale for what became one of the most highly politicized and transparently unfair transformations in national policy in modern memory. Their unfortunate legacy remains to this day—and with it, the perilous progress of the profession they represent.[6]

6. M.A. Bernstein, *A Perilous Progress: Economists and Public Purpose in Twentieth-Century America* (Princeton: Princeton University Press, 2001), p. 147.

Turning inward to find comfort in scholarly detachment, many of the supply-siders' colleagues could not bring themselves to speak out in opposition. As the economics profession rapidly retreated from the public role it had once coveted, it became more and more a mouthpiece for market-driven, business-oriented solutions that shunned government intervention and venerated private wealth. Problems and issues relating to those who, by intention or otherwise, had benefited from government intervention, such as the poor, were more and more ignored. Economic theory followed, distancing itself farther and farther from reality. The Council of Economic Advisers that once represented an unchallenged repository of economic skills enlisted for public service and open discussion was reduced to a virtually invisible collection of bankers and ideologically conservative economists. It also lost political support and came under Congressional threat of elimination. Here the profession sits today, with the irrelevance of large portions of its research to the fundamental issues facing the American economy exposed and glaring. Of course, there has been some promising movement by establishment economics in the directions of inquiry pursued by radical economists, as will be described at the beginning of Chapter 9 and, in addition, into new areas such as behavioral and experimental economics. But as was the case in the late 1920s with respect to the Great Depression, the profession generally did not foresee or recognize the Great Recession until well after it had begun in January of 2008, and was as unprepared for dealing with that recession as it was for the Great Depression eight decades earlier.

* * *

It should be observed, however, that the suppression of deviant ideas pursued over the years by the economics establishment was never complete. There have always been dissenters, albeit relegated to the margins of the discipline, challenging the conventional view. For example, the Union for Radical Political Economics was formed at a meeting in Ann Arbor, Michigan in the summer of 1968 (the same summer in which Vietnam War protests culminated in the large demonstrations at the Democratic presidential-nominating convention in Chicago) to further left-leaning critiques of, and alternatives to the establishment view of economics.[7] Its journal, the *Review of Radical Political Economics* began publication shortly thereafter. But as was made clear earlier, the establishment was sufficiently well rooted and equipped to easily fend off such dissenters' attacks.

Nevertheless, if the left-leaning dissent had little influence in the economics establishment, it was still spread all over the map. Yale, Stanford, and Harvard Universities will serve as illustrations.[8] In the early 1970s a significant number of graduate students at Yale pressured the economics faculty to offer courses in Marxian economics and other radical- or political-economy-related topics. The token response by the Economics Department was to offer grudgingly a few such courses, some taught by an advanced graduate student and later by an assistant professor who, it would turn out, would not be given tenure. (The assistant professor, David Levine, was the same person as the graduate student, who had received his PhD and

---

7. For a discussion of the founding of the Union for Radical Political Economics and its early years, see T. Mata and F.S. Lee, "The Role of Oral History in the Historiography of Heterodox Economics," in *Economists' Lives: Biography and Autobiography in the History of Economics*, E.R. Weintraub and E.L. Forget, eds. (Durham: Duke University Press, 2007), pp. 154–171.

8. For additional details on the events at Yale, Stanford, and Harvard, see L.S. Lifschultz, "Could Karl Marx Teach Economics in America?" *Ramparts* 12, 9 (April, 1974):28–30, 53–56. This paragraph and the next rely heavily on that same source. See also T. Mata, "Migrations and Boundary Work: Harvard, Radical Economists, and the Committee on Political Discrimination," *Science in Context* 22, 1 (2009): 115–143.

been away from Yale for a year.) Stanford University actually had a tenured Marxist faculty member, Paul Baran, in its Economics Department until he died in 1964. But he was harassed in a variety of ways, including increased teaching loads and no salary raises. For the present story, however, it is the events at Harvard University that were of major significance.

In 1969 there were five radical economists in the Harvard Economics Department. But contrary to what this might suggest, that department was not favorably disposed toward radical political economy. Only one of the radicals had been given tenure and, in his case, tenure had been granted on the basis of orthodox economic work before his research had turned in radical directions. During the fall semester of the 1972–1973 academic year, in a highly controversial decision, the Department denied Samuel S. Bowles, an untenured associate professor, promotion to full professor with tenure. Bowles, recall, was a radical economist who had written about the economics of U.S. education and how that education had historically reproduced certain class relationships in American society. Three well-known past presidents of the American Economic Association, John K. Galbraith, Wassily Leontief, and Kenneth J. Arrow (the latter two were also economics Nobel laureates), supported the promotion. However, the senior faculty voting as a whole turned him down. Those in the majority claimed Bowles's work was not up to Harvard's professional standards; the minority opinion was that promotion was refused for political reasons. At the same time, another of the untenured radical economists was denied reappointment. These two decisions prompted the Harvard graduate students to decry what they saw as the evasion by the economics faculty of any discussion of the evils of capitalism, such as the maintenance and repression of a poor underclass in American society, and the eviction of any one who would consider those evils. The criticisms of the students and the faculty who supported Bowles led the Economics Department to attempt a compromise by offering Herbert Gintis an assistant professorship for the next year with a guaranteed promotion to a nontenured associate professorship the following year. Gintis, one of the five radical economists mentioned earlier, had been a lecturer in the Department in 1969–1970. Although, at that time, the Department voted against promoting him to assistant professor, he nevertheless succeeded in obtaining an assistant professor position in Harvard's School of Education. Now he was offered, after one year as an assistant professor in the Economics Department, promotion to associate professor in that department. But along with that offer, Gintis was informally told that there was no future possibility of tenure or promotion to full professor in the Department if he continued his participation in radical politics at Harvard.[9] Be that as it may, Gintis accepted the 1973–1974 assistant professorship, and both Bowles and Gintis left Harvard for the University of Massachusetts at Amherst the following year to take up positions there in the fall of 1974. Upon their departure, the only radical economist left in the Harvard Economics Department was the one who had tenure.

The controversy surrounding the radical economists at Harvard spilled over into the economics profession at large. At the American Economics Association's annual meeting held in Toronto in late December of 1972, a resolution was proposed condemning past actions, purportedly like that of the Harvard economics faculty,

9. In April of 1969, Harvard students led by the Harvard Chapter of the Students for a Democratic Society (SDS) went on strike and occupied University Hall in protest of the Vietnam War. Because he was a member of the Strike Steering Committee of the local SDS Chapter (Gintis had supported the strike but not the takeover of University Hall), the Harvard Board of Overseers ordered that Gintis be dismissed from taking up the fall-1969 lecturer position to which had been appointed by the Economics Department. However, he was reinstated by the Department in time for the fall of 1969.

that denied tenure and reappointment to radical economists due to political bias or lack of familiarity with their work. The resolution that was finally adopted, however, did not acknowledge that such bias had actually occurred, and only condemned the general possibility of "... political discrimination in hiring decisions against radical economists or any others."[10] But as might be deduced from earlier discussion in this chapter, the resolution had virtually no impact on the general attitude of the economics profession toward dissent. Moreover, approximately one year later on December 10 and 11 of 1973, a committee appointed by the Harvard University administration visited Harvard's Economics Department for the purpose of providing a general evaluation of that department. In the visiting committee's report of April 15, 1974, the chairman of the Department, James S. Dusenberry, is quoted as arguing that there was no bias in the Bowles tenure decision and that radical economics was not sufficiently significant within the discipline of economics to outweigh claims to resources for hiring in other areas.[11] And one member of the visiting committee wrote,

> The division of opinion over Bowles involved only a small minority... and represented the sort of difference of opinion that any large faculty might expect to have. Had it not been for the size and intensity of the reaction from graduate students, nothing much would have followed from the Bowles decision.[12]

Like its impact on the attitude toward dissent of the economics profession at large, the dispute over radical economists at Harvard

10. Minutes of the Annual Meeting, *American Economic Review* 63 (May, 1973): 472–473.
11. A.F. Brimmer. (committee chairman), "Report of the Committee to Visit the Department of Economics," April 15, 1973, pp. 28–29.
12. Ibid., p. 14.

had little effect on the hiring and tenure policies of that university's Economics Department.

The story of the move by Bowles and Gintis to Amherst will be told in Chapter 6. But for now, two issues need to be addressed. First, why did the most important and visible assemblage of academic radical economists created in the United States up to that time find a home at the University of Massachusetts at Amherst and not some other place? There seem to have been at least four elements that came together to play an important role in producing such a result: (1) The University, although nearing the end of an expansionary phase (recall Chapter 2), still had positions available that it could fill with economists. (2) The rejection of radical political economy by the economics establishment made it relatively easy to recruit radical economics faculty. Indeed, as will be described more fully later, it was the denial of promotion and tenure to Bowles by the Harvard Economics Department that set in motion the process of establishing a radical contingent at the University of Massachusetts. (3) The turmoil on university campuses in general during the two-year period 1972–1973, along with the efforts (not present on many other college campuses) by the University of Massachusetts administration to accommodate student demands as much as possible and hopefully, thereby, to minimize the likelihood (as suggested in Chapter 3) that the protests on the Amherst campus would get out of hand, left the administration open to the possibility of hiring radical economists. In addition to civil rights and Vietnam War protests, Amherst campus students were also demonstrating in support of a radical faculty member who was threatened with termination of his appointment by the University's Economics Department. Moreover, the number of economics majors was very low, further suggesting possible students' desires for a greater diversity, especially on the left where protesters' sympathies lay, of economic views on

THE AMERICAN ECONOMICS PROFESSION

campus. Thus, as long as academic standards could be maintained, the hiring of the radical economists could have been seen by the administration as a move that would win student approval. And it would certainly bolster the case for going forward to know that the students would be on the administration's side. Again, the details will be filled in later on. (4) As indicated in Chapter 2, the state of Massachusetts left the University alone and did not interfere in the hiring and keeping of a sizable number of radical economists. This last factor, of course, is rather important since the University of Massachusetts is a public, not private institution.

The second issue relates to the factors that led to the formation of a radical subculture within the economics profession. These appear to be at least twofold: On the one hand, as related in Chapter 3 and apart from those who grew up as "red diaper babies"[13] and were already following a radical path, participation in, or observation of, the civil rights movement and Vietnam War protests deeply disturbed and radicalized many young people in very general ways. On the other, the economics profession was, at the same time, beginning to experience its fall from grace with the start of simultaneous inflation and unemployment that neoclassical economic theory could not explain. In confluence with that fall, the profession's relegation, as described earlier, of real-world problems like poverty to the dust bin of economics was well under way. It was quite natural, then, for young economists who grew up radical or who had been radicalized to direct their intellectual attentions to alternative systems of economic thought and to take up the banner of what they considered to

13. Red diaper babies are children whose parents were members of, or sympathetic to the aims of, the Communist Party in the United States. Although Communism was relatively popular in the United States during the 1930s, its popularity waned considerably after World War II. By the 1970s most red diaper babies would have been anywhere between 20 and 50 years of age.

75

be neglected but still fundamental and important issues. The stubborn rejection by the economics establishment of any alternatives to its neoclassical approach to economic analysis and to its highly restricted and narrow view of the nature of the questions and issues that are relevant to the subject of economics only served to push them further from the mainstream.

Consider, for example, the conversion to the radical economics fold of three of the University of Massachusetts faculty members mentioned in Chapter 1. First, Samuel S. Bowles[14] grew up in an environment of democratic political liberalism, fair-mindedness, tolerance, and activism. His early years were spent in rural New England and India, the latter (1951–1953) as a result of his father's, Chester B. Bowles, appointment as United States Ambassador to India and Nepal by President Harry S. Truman. Attending public school in Delhi, he considered himself average among his classmates and wondered why India was so poor relative to the United States when peoples' capacities in the two countries were so similar. The latter concern with poverty was reinforced during a two-year stint as a high school teacher in a remote area of Nigeria. Like many economists, Bowles was drawn to economics because he thought it might provide insight into the alleviation of poverty and the conditions under which a free people might grow and prosper.[15] He enrolled in Harvard as a graduate student and obtained a thorough

---

14. See P. Arestis and M. Sawyer, eds., *A Biographical Dictionary of Dissenting Economists*, 2nd. ed. (Cheltenham: Elgar, 2000), pp. 73–75, and S. Bowles, *Microeconomics: Behavior, Institutions*, and *Evolution* (New York: Russell Sage Foundation, 2004), p. 7.

15. In his *Microeconomics: Behavior, Institutions, and Evolution* (New York: Russell Sage Foundation, 2004), p. 7, Bowles cites an introductory passage in Alfred Marshall's *Principles of Economics*, 8th ed. (New York: Macmillan, 1948), p. 3, where Marshall wrote, "... we are setting ourselves seriously to inquire ... whether there need be large numbers of people doomed from their birth to hard work in order to provide for others the requisites of a refined and cultured life; while they themselves are prevented by their poverty and toil from having any share or part in that life."

education in neoclassical economics. Bowles received his PhD in 1965 and immediately joined the Harvard faculty to teach advanced microeconomics at the graduate level.[16] However, as a newly hired faculty member, he refused to sign the oath of loyalty to the U.S. constitution required by Massachusetts law as a condition for teaching in the state, was fired, and then reinstated after a successful legal campaign in which the law was declared unconstitutional by the Massachusetts Supreme Judicial Court. He was to remain on the Harvard economics faculty until 1973.

Meanwhile, in the mid 1960s, with the civil rights movement at its peak and the Vietnam War protests escalating, the gap between the poverty issues in which he was interested (and that he considered to be among the most important economic issues of the day) and those addressed from the neoclassical perspective had, in his mind, become so great that Bowles (along with a number of colleagues at Harvard) decided he needed to turn in a new direction. With others, he wrote background papers for Martin Luther King's poor people's march in 1968. He became involved in the Vietnam War protest movement. During this period, Bowles came to believe that, whatever its past accomplishments, capitalism, for then and for the future, was and would be a failure as an economic system that was supposed to contribute to human betterment. The theoretical underpinning of capitalism, namely neoclassical economics, was useless or worse. Moreover, capitalism had been embraced by American-style liberalism and there were other facets of that liberalism that also had to be abandoned, namely, its failure to uphold liberty and national sovereignty. As Bowles saw things, the failure to uphold liberty was evidenced by the fact that several of the

16. He subsequently published a well-received book on neoclassical economics with David A. Kendrick based on the material he taught: *Notes and Problems in Microeconomic Theory* (Chicago: Markham, 1970).

AT THE EDGE OF CAMELOT

proponents of American-style liberalism had urged him to sign the loyalty oath that he, as noted earlier, had rejected. Their support of the war in Vietnam was interpreted as a denial of that country's national sovereignty. In Bowles's view, democratic socialism was the modern expression of the Enlightenment and the liberal tradition. His political orientation, therefore, moved to the left and he turned to Marxism because it seemed to provide a means to address the economic issues with which he was concerned.

The second faculty member, James R. Crotty, describes his conversion to radical economics as follows:[17]

Many of us came to radical economics through the anti-war movement of the late 1960s and early 1970s. Some of us also participated in the civil rights movement —I did not. I took my first teaching job at the State University of New York at Buffalo in 1966 before completing my Ph.D. degree at Carnegie Mellon University. At that time I had no formal political perspective or ideology. I did, however, have strong working class instincts, so I knew where my sympathies lay; and I also knew that I was totally alienated from the neoclassical economic theory I had been taught at Carnegie. (Most of my education there seemed to me to be mathematical games, which I liked and was pretty good at, about abstract problems having no obvious connection to anything important to people. There were no course offerings in either economic history or the history of economic thought. These subjects were both considered unnecessary, the latter being the description of a long struggle to overcome one error after another that, in the early 1960s, finally arrived at the "truth." And who needs to study error?) Almost immediately I got

---

17. From a document attached to e-mail correspondence dated June, 8, 2006. Included here with permission.

caught up in the movement against the Vietnam War and began to read non-mainstream political economy and Marxist thought in an attempt to understand why this tragedy was taking place. I became an activist at the State University of New York at Buffalo and was genuinely shocked when I first came to realize that I had become a leftist—the kind of person I had been taught as a kid educated in Catholic schools to hate. I began to believe that economics was crucially important; that we needed a thorough understanding of it in order to build valid theories that could help explain why the world was the way it was and how we might change it for the better. And I considered Marx to be a wonderful source of insights about capitalism. I abandoned a dissertation that was three-fourths completed on structural and empirical aspects of neoclassical investment theory and started over, investigating Marxian class conflict and its implications for macroeconomic policy. Because it was outside of what the economics establishment considered to be economics, this topic generated some controversy at Carnegie and approval of my dissertation was delayed. However, I was no longer alienated from economic theory. I had become really excited about it. But, of course, it was non-neoclassical, Marxian-inspired economic theory that I was excited about.

Finally, Stephen A. Resnick's experience was not very dissimilar from that of Bowles and Crotty. Early on, Marxism was a part of discussions with family and family friends that evolved around the Communist takeover in China (1949), the Korean War, and the cold war. These discussions also touched on economics and were responsible for kindling an interest in both that subject and Marxism. Although informally mentioned in graduate school at Massachusetts Institute of Technology, Marxian notions, such as exploitation and class struggle, were, much to Resnick's disappointment, not a part of its neoclassical and Keynesian curriculum.[18] Resnick, however, thoroughly enjoyed and appreciated his education at MIT. However, as an assistant professor on Yale University's faculty, he was later to become disenchanted with its neoclassical and Keynesian content. While at Yale, Resnick spent a year living in the Philippines, and he could not believe the severity and extensiveness of the poverty he had encountered. Upon his return, the impact of the Vietnam War and its seemingly endless continuation also began to weigh on him. He became involved in the Vietnam War protest movement. He began serious intellectual interactions with colleagues and individuals who had similar feelings. Very little in his education at MIT appeared to address the poverty and war issues that now loomed so importantly in his mind. And Marxism seemed to provide a way to understand them. His prior interest in Marxism naturally led him in this new, radical direction. Resnick left Yale for City College of New York in the spring of 1971, early in the period (mentioned earlier) during which Yale's economics faculty began to offer a few courses in political-economy-related and Marxian economics.

These three stories of transformation were not unusual. Many others, engaging both faculty and graduate students, fit into comparable molds.

18. The Keynesianism referred to here was that relating to the neoclassical synthesis mentioned in Chapter 1.

Chapter 5

The Kindahl Era

The previous three chapters have provided background information relating to the University of Massachusetts at Amherst, the economics profession, and the social, political, and cultural environment in the United States that is necessary for any understanding of how the creation of a group of radical economists within the University's Economics Department took place. It is to that latter development that attention now turns. To describe it and the events that followed, it is appropriate to begin with the initial attempt by the University to transform its Economics Department into one of prominence and repute.

During the 1960s the University, as indicated in Chapter 2, was undergoing a period of considerable expansion and transformation. This was seen by the administration as an opportunity to create an accomplished faculty in place of one that had very weak academic credentials. The administration's strategy within each field was to recruit a strong leader as department head, a position endowed with pretty much full authority over hiring and other personnel decisions, and charge him with the responsibility of rebuilding. Research was to become a high priority and faculty democracy, which might precipitate opposition to action taken by the head, was to be suppressed. The strategy paid off, and there was considerable improvement in the quality of the faculty. However, by the late 1960s, many faculty members, including some of those who had been hired by the new heads, had become restive and dissatisfied with the authoritarian environment in which they lived and worked. The result was a movement toward democratization that will be described later.

In the early 1960s, it will be recalled, the humanities and fine arts, mathematics and the natural sciences, and the social and behavioral sciences were all a part of a unified College of Arts and Sciences headed by a single dean. That dean was I. Moyer Hunsberger, a chemist, who had come to the University in 1960 as head of the Chemistry Department, and who was appointed dean in the spring of 1961. The provost on this occasion was a botanist, Oswald Tippo. At the time of Hunsberger's appointment to the deanship, the Economics Department, in Hunsberger's words of a few years later, "had absolutely no stature in the [economics] profession."[1] The head of the Department was still Phillip L. Gamble who, over the years, had become a popular teacher.[2] Desiring to build a major department, and believing that change could ensue only with new leadership, Hunsberger put pressure on Gamble to resign the headship position. That resignation came in February of 1964.

But Hunsberger quickly found that it was not going to be easy to build a major Economics Department at the University of Massachusetts. "At first, I had the naive hope that...some capable Head of Department could be attracted by our enormous potential to come here and recruit an outstanding faculty. What I learned the hard way was that our stature was too low and the market was too 'tight' to permit this solution to our problem."[3] Between February of 1964 and December of 1967 the Economics Department had two different acting heads, and three different search committees

1. Hunsberger's memo to Provost Tippo of December 4, 1967, p. 1.
2. As was pointed out in Chapter 2, Gamble joined the Department soon after it was created in 1935 and became its head in 1942.
3. Hunsberger's memo to Provost Tippo of December 4, 1967, p. 1.

had attempted and failed to find a suitable and permanent replacement for Gamble. Not surprisingly, tensions were rising between Hunsberger and the Department. In recognition of these difficulties, Hunsberger, during the fall of 1966, brought in a team of three well-known economists, Robert M. Solow (MIT), George H. Borts (Brown University), and Lawrence R. Klein (University of Pennsylvania) to evaluate the Economics Department and advise him about what to do.

The report of that committee, received in January of 1967, acknowledged that the Department was understaffed, that the faculty was engaged in little or no research, that there was sentiment among the faculty for dropping the PhD program (a program that would be essential if the Department were to improve its stature), that there was no leadership within the Department, that related departments wanted to see the Economics Department improved, and that improvement would not come without the commitment of substantial sums of money and initiative from outside the Department. The report recommended, among other things, that a strong head be appointed along with five additional persons, all of whom combine both teaching and research; that "the deplorable state of present research activity should not be allowed to continue"; and that the PhD program not be terminated. The report also contained the following statement:[4]

It is a familiar academic problem for an institution to be saddled with professors on tenure who are obstacles to department development and out of touch with current thinking in their professional fields. The administration and department must face the challenge

---

4. Report of the Committee of Consultants on the Department of Economics, January 11, 1967, p. 5 (date written by hand).

of such personnel and not be deterred by their presence. We offer no solution to this difficult situation except to suggest that such people be given academic assignments that remove them as far as possible from the main work of departmental reconstruction.

The report concludes by identifying potential candidates for appointment to the positions it recommends. The lead name on its list was Vernon L. Smith who was then a professor of Economics at Purdue University. Smith was one of the most original economists of the time. He was at the height of his powers and was moving in a direction that would eventually win him the Nobel Prize in economics.

With the resignation of Gamble, Bruce R. Morris was appointed acting head. He remained so until September 1968—except for the 1965–1966 academic year when he was the recipient of a Fulbright grant to teach at the University of Baghdad in Iraq. During his year away, Marshall C. Howard took his place as acting head. The twenty- month period following the receipt of the report of the evaluation committee saw the addition of ten faculty members to the Economics Department, a substantial number of whom already were, or turned out to be, active scholars publishing their work in major economics outlets. Included in this group of new recruits, all but one having arrived on campus by September 1967, were Smith (full professor) and James K. Kindahl (associate professor). Smith did not appear until September 1968. In the recruiting of these people, especially Smith and Kindahl, Hunsberger seems to have played a major role. Smith, who at that time was visiting Brown University, wanted to be located near his wife's Unitarian pulpit outside Boston. Brown and MIT were showing interest in appointing him on a permanent basis. But, according to Hunsberger, Smith preferred a state university to the Ivy League and was intrigued by the prospect, promised by Hunsberger, of building a Department to his liking.[5]

Kindahl was attracted to the University of Massachusetts by the bucolic characteristics of the physical environment in Amherst. But he was also interested in the possibilities associated with building up the Economics Department. A highly principled man of considerable integrity, and a mainstream economist with substantial statistical background and skill, Kindahl received his PhD from the University of Chicago and was known for his work with George J. Stigler on industrial prices. He taught at Johns Hopkins University, Amherst College, and the University of Chicago before settling at the University of Massachusetts. After one year in the Economics Department as an associate professor, he was promoted by Hunsberger to professor and head of the Department in September of 1968. In accepting the position of head, Kindahl was committed to following the direction set out by Hunsberger. The two men had great admiration and respect for each other. It was agreed that Kindahl would do what was necessary to transform Economics into a major department, and Hunsberger, assuming the appropriate justifications were forthcoming, would back him with full monetary and administrative support. There were, of course, implicit limits imposed on the size and budget of the Department. But, for many practical purposes, Hunsberger gave Kindahl considerable free rein.

Kindahl set out his plans for the development of the Economics Department in several written statements. The content of those statements included the following:[6] The Economics Department has responsibilities for both graduate and undergraduate teaching, and

5. Ibid., pp. 3–4.
6. Subsequent material is taken from Kindahl's statements on plans dated October 14, 1969 and November, 1970.

James K. Kindahl, August, 1968. *(Courtesy of Special Collections and University Archives, W.E.B. Du Bois Library, University of Massachusetts at Amherst)*

the obligation to contribute to the development of the profession through research. Areas of research that are important in the profession should be represented in the Department. One very important area in which the Department was especially weak was economic theory, much of which was (and still is) constructed and expressed in mathematical form. In addition to economic theory, substantive fields of application, involving, in part, statistical analyses are also important. However, no plan or system of priorities should ever be allowed to prevent the hiring of first-rate people regardless of field or approach. Successful teaching and research go hand-in-hand; a person cannot be successful at one or the other without engaging in both. On occasion, the Department may make additional time available for an individual's research by temporarily reducing his teaching load. In one of the earlier statements, Kindahl also made a promise:[7]

7. Statement of Plans for the Development of the Department of Economics, October 14, 1969, p. 5.

> In the Department as I envision it in the future, there is room for
> people with the interests and approaches of everyone now on the
> staff. No member of the faculty will be discriminated against by
> me in matters of promotions, tenure, or merit [salary] increases
> because of his field of interest or approach to economics. I shall do
> my best to judge each individual on the quality of work done in the
> classroom and in research.

This promise may have been, to some extent, a response to the tension in the Department that, as partly anticipated in the quotation
from the 1967 aforementioned evaluation report, was growing.
Even so, Kindahl sincerely believed (as did Smith) that the pursuit
of knowledge and scholarship was the main mission of a University
and, as the preceding quotation suggests, he was quite open to alternative methodologies and ideologies. Kindahl also was helpful to
and supportive of younger faculty whom he thought had significant
scholarly potential.

Recruiting during Kindahl's first year as head of the Department
(1968–1969), resulted in twenty offers being extended to economists at all ranks. However, only four of those made at the lowest
ranks were accepted.

Citing personal reasons, Hunsberger resigned the position of
dean of the College of Arts and Sciences on March 1, 1969 and was
replaced by Acting Dean Seymour Shapiro, a botanist. By that time
the College had more than doubled in size and the need for its reorganization had become clear. Discussion centered on breaking up
the College into smaller groups, one of which would be comprised
of only the social and behavioral sciences. Kindahl was concerned
about the effect this change might have on the efforts to build the
Economics Department. Shapiro held the same attitude toward
the Department as Hunsberger and had continued Hunsberger's

financial and administrative support. But in any reorganization of the sort under consideration, the Economics Department would be unlikely to remain in the same unit over which Shapiro or a replacement from the physical sciences would be positioned as dean. In a handwritten draft of a memo sent to Shapiro in April of 1969, Kindahl worried that a new dean coming from the social and behavioral sciences might not be as sympathetic to the building process. Kindahl's fears probably arose from the fact that, by this time, academic economists had begun to think of economics as a science that imitated the methods employed in the physical sciences. This had set in motion a movement toward the extensive use of mathematics and statistics in economics. The other social and behavioral sciences were lagging behind, if not completely rejecting this trend. And Kindahl may have thought that a dean drawn from one of those areas would not, due to a background exhibiting some resistance to mathematics, appreciate as much as Shapiro the direction in which economics was going.

At the same time, in response to the growth of faculty dissatisfaction with the lack of democracy in the running of the University, the faculty senate was clarifying the form that faculty participation should have in University governance. A report of a subcommittee on the role of the faculty in University decision making presented in April of 1969 stated the general principles. These included the following:[8] There should be faculty participation at all levels of University government, including the department level. Although general practice at the University had been to have department heads rather than department chairmen or, for short, chairs (the distinction between a head and a chair will be indicated momentarily), the latter form of organization should be available if a department

8. Senate Document 69–044, pp. 14, 24–25.

wanted to govern itself that way. However, because there may be departments that are judged unable to govern themselves effectively with a chair, the provost would still have the power to overrule a department decision in favor of the chair system and appoint a strong head. Motions supporting these principles were approved by the senate in early May and sent to the trustees for consideration. The distinction between a head and a chair contained in the motions was later summarized by Provost Tippo's successor:

> The basic distinction between a Head and a Chairman is understood to turn on the question of where the responsibility for administrative recommendations lies. In the case of a Head, the recommending initiative lies with the Head, with advisory faculty votes accompanying the Head's recommendations. In the case of a Chairman, it is the vote of the faculty [or a designated faculty committee] which governs the departmental recommendation, with the Chairman's opinion accompanying the departmental recommendation.[9]

In the handwritten draft memo to Shapiro just cited, along with his fear that a social or behavioral science dean might not be supportive of the Economics Department's building program, Kindahl was further concerned that increased faculty democracy within the Economics Department as set out by the senate might also impede the Department's growth and development. In a formal memo to Provost Tippo the following December 22, 1969 he was more precise about the latter:

> In my view, immediate implementation of the [more democratic, i.e., chair] form of government...would doom the Department of

9. Memo from Provost Gluckstern, September 28, 1970 (Document P71–F7).

Economics to a permanent state of mediocrity. The Department has not yet reached the point where "faculty democracy" could be relied on to make the critical and difficult decisions which must be made within the next few years.... I have seen no evidence which would lead me to believe that a majority of the present Department could agree on a coherent plan of development and then implement it with the judgment and determination necessary to bring success.[10]

However, in April of 1970, the University's board of trustees approved in principle the recommendations of the faculty senate on faculty participation in university government, and, in August of that year, it approved the division of the College of Arts and Sciences into three faculties: Humanities and Fine Arts, Natural Sciences and Mathematics, and Social and Behavioral Sciences, each with its own administration and dean. On September 1, 1970, Jeremiah Allen, a professor of English, replaced Shapiro as acting dean of the College of Arts and Sciences until the new structure, including the appointment of new deans, could be put into place. Several months earlier, Robert L. Gluckstern, a physicist, had taken over as provost from Tippo who had moved up to the position of chancellor.

During the 1969–1970 academic year, in the environment created by the discussion and passage of the faculty senate's motions on university governance, tensions within the Economics Department continued to grow. In addition to those who favored greater democracy, some faculty members, especially those without tenure, may have felt threatened by the new emphasis on research

10. Interestingly, whereas the radical political economists who replaced many of the establishment or mainstream economists hired by Kindahl (see Chapter 6) saw power as necessary to make change, mainstream economists like Kindahl tended to play down the role of power in their understanding of the economic world. It is ironic, then, that Kindahl believed that the use of administrative power by a head, and the rejection of the democracy inherent in the chair form of governance, was necessary to change the Economics Department.

and by Kindahl's efforts to build an academically significant department. (Kindahl had recommended that a faculty member be denied tenure in November of 1969.) But more departmental faculty than just those without tenure were resisting Kindahl and his policies. In the fall, some faculty members demanded input beyond that of an advisory role in recruitment and its direction. Kindahl, who had full authority to recommend appointments by dint of his position as head, made significant concessions. However, these were insufficient to satisfy those who were requesting greater participation. Early in the Spring Semester, there were two faculty resignations, one from the position of assistant head of the Department (he remained a faculty member) and the other severing his connection to the University entirely. The reasons cited for the resignations were alienation and Departmental turmoil in the first instance, and changed departmental and University priorities in the second. Kindahl had to defend his positions on the undergraduate program and on the maintenance of the graduate program to both the Department and the administration. Finally, at a Department faculty meeting on May 7, 1970, after the trustees had approved the faculty senate's recommendations on faculty participation in University governance, the Department voted 13 to 5, over Kindahl's objections, to change the organization of the Department by replacing the position of head by that of a chair. At the same meeting, the faculty voted to establish an executive committee as a further aspect of Department reorganization. The executive committee would handle matters of policy and administration that were not already delegated to the personnel and other committees. The executive committee actually met twice (Kindahl, who was supposed to be present, would not attend) before the reorganization was stopped by Acting Dean Shapiro and Provost Gluckstern in June.

First, the dean and provost refused to change Kindahl's status from head to chair. Second, they decided to bring in a visiting review committee to evaluate the Department's strengths and weaknesses and to make recommendations for future growth and development. Third, Provost Gluckstern asked the Department to withdraw its request for the change from head to chair and reconsider it after the visiting committee delivered its report. The Department acquiesced and rescinded its vote to replace the head by a chair in a faculty meeting on October 14, 1970. It is remarkable that, in spite of these goings on, the Department still made significant progress in recruiting during 1969–1970: Twelve offers were extended and six were accepted. Included in the group of acceptees were several microeconomic theorists with mathematical backgrounds of various strengths. But serious damage to Kindahl's ability to lead the Department had been inflicted.

The most impressive scholar among that incoming group was one of the more mathematically oriented persons among them: Hugo F. Sonnenschein. Sonnenschein had already made significant contributions to microeconomic theory and was in the midst of a project that was destined to have a major impact on microeconomic general equilibrium theory.[11] Eventually he would become President of the University of Chicago. Although he had declined an offer to join the Department the previous year, he subsequently changed his mind, having been lured by Kindahl and Smith and the opportunity to be involved in the building of the Department, by the prospect of being better located with respect to family, and by the attractiveness of the Amherst area.

---

11. Microeconomic general equilibrium theory concerns the simultaneous, interactive behavior of consumers, firms, and markets in determining prices and quantities throughout the microeconomy.

By the end of October, 1970, the Faculty of Social and Behavioral Sciences had been separated from the College of Arts and Sciences, and a permanent dean of the former had been appointed. The new dean was a political scientist by the name of Dean Alfange, Jr. Alfange had not been an obvious candidate for the deanship. This was the time when campuses across the country were in turmoil because of student (and often faculty) opposition to the Vietnam War. Students were demanding, and in many cases receiving, a greater role in the decision-making procedures of their institutions. Activism at the University of Massachusetts, which, as indicated in Chapter 3, had now caught up to that in the rest of the country, was intense. The leading candidate to be the first dean of the Faculty of Social and Behavioral Science was an outspoken supporter of the war and contemptuous of its critics. Student hostility toward him was considerable and ended the possibility of his appointment as dean. Alfange was young. But he was well known on campus and thought of as a moderate, and Gluckstern appointed him to the dean position.

Dean Alfange, Jr., February, 1971. (*Courtesy of Special Collections and University Archives, W.E.B. Du Bois Library, University of Massachusetts at Amherst*)

The visiting review committee that had been promised by Shapiro and Gluckstern arrived on campus during the fall of 1970. Two of its members, Solow and Klein, had been on the earlier 1967 evaluation committee. The remaining members were James Tobin (Yale), Robert Heilbroner (New School for Social Research), and William Capron (associate dean of the Kennedy School of Government at Harvard). The committee's report of January 1971 began by noting the enormous and obvious improvement in the Department over the previous four years. "We believe," the report went on, "that the Economics Department can and should aim for parity with the great state universities of the midwest (Ann Arbor, Wisconsin, Minnesota). This requires a faculty which is making recognized contributions to the mainstream of professional research." Later on the report focuses on recent and current hiring:

> As a result of the successful recruitment program of the past three years, the Department has clearly established a strong base in one of the core areas of economics, rigorous microeconomic theory. Especially if...[a current outstanding offer]...is accepted, the Department will have...a core group of quality comparable to the best departments in the country. They can be expected to make the University of Massachusetts an important center of theoretical research, and to make a strong contribution to the teaching of graduate students and advanced undergraduates.

There was, of course, an implicit assumption in the report that those who the committee identified as quality economists would remain permanently as faculty of the Department. But it turned out that the offer referred to was not accepted and the "core group of quality" was essentially gone within two years.

The hires of the previous year had left the Department with a heavy emphasis on microeconomic theory.[12] However, many of those who had pushed for a more democratic departmental administration also favored greater diversity. In particular, the opposition to Kindahl, in their presentations to the visiting review committee, emphasized the lack of macroeconomists in the Economics Department. Kindahl, to be sure, had no difficulty in attempting to recruit economists of this type. During the 1968–1969 hiring season, three of the twenty offers he had extended went to monetary economists.[13] All three offers, however, had been rejected. The efforts by Kindahl to hire monetary (and other) economists notwithstanding, the lack of diversity in the Department at the time was noted by the visiting review committee. For another aspect of their report was its recommendation that the Department should now concentrate on diversifying into areas that were not adequately represented. In the committee's opinion, the most critical need in this regard was macroeconomic theory and policy, and the report suggests that a major recruiting effort to eliminate the gap was needed. After that, the Department should add persons in other areas as the opportunities present themselves and distinguished people become available.

Finally, the report addressed the divisions and tensions within the Department. It began this discussion with brief but considerable praise for Kindahl:

James Kindahl deserves enormous personal credit for the progress already made by the Department. Nevertheless, the fact must

---

12. It is interesting that Kindahl, a statistician and econometrician who had little personal interest in microeconomic theory, pursued and successfully recruited a number of highly active microeconomic theorists.

13. There is considerable overlap in terms of their interests and what they do between macroeconomists and monetary economists. Indeed, they are often considered to be substitutes for one another.

be faced that today there is deep division among the members of the Department.... [This is probably]...an inevitable concomitant of rapid progress, given the desperate condition in which the Department began....In our judgment, it is unlikely that Professor Kindahl can reestablish himself as an effective leader of this Department....However, we caution against abrupt action now. The time to make a change in leadership is when a new head of department can be recruited from outside. In the meanwhile, it is important that the University Administration back Professor Kindahl.

The report goes on to give reasons for retaining Kindahl as Department head. These included (1) that there were still some faculty that had to be let go, and it would be better that Kindahl did this rather than burden a new incoming head with the tensions that might be aroused, and (2) that this would clearly show that the University is fully committed to the academic excellence "so strongly associated with Professor Kindahl's leadership." Nevertheless, the preceding passage of the report could still be read in two ways: On the one hand, it might be interpreted to mean that Kindahl should be replaced as soon as an appropriate substitute from outside the Department could be found. On the other, it is possible to be read as asserting that, for now, the administration should fully back Kindahl to give him time to put more of his rebuilding program in place.

But there was another matter that was to have, at least in the long run, even greater significance than the internal battles within the Department and the visiting committee's report. In his first year as Department head, Kindahl had recruited Michael H. Best, a new PhD from the University of Oregon. Best joined the Department in the fall of 1969 with a two-year, tenure-track appointment at the rank of assistant professor. Best, it turned out, was a radical political

Michael H. Best, November, 1980. *(Courtesy of Special Collections and University Archives, W.E.B. Du Bois Library, University of Massachusetts at Amherst)*

economist (or, for short, a political economist or just a radical). In its aims and content, radical political economy was, as described earlier, on the periphery of the academic economics profession, some distance from the academic economics establishment. Its basic concerns at the start of the 1960s were with inequality and imperialism. Believing that the standard approaches to economics at the time were inadequate and irrelevant to addressing these topics, the radicals turned to the writings of Marx and other nonorthodox economists. During the 1960s radical thought evolved so that, at its core, emerged the notion of class as it related to Marxian and various reformulations of Marxian analyses. However, apart from the unity represented by that core, the radicals were still sharply divided on many methodological, theoretical, and empirical issues.

It is not clear if Kindahl knew of Best's radicalism when the latter was hired. If Kindahl did know, he may have underestimated the full significance of its implications. All the same, Best had made no effort to hide his radical interests. Moreover, his doctoral dissertation did make use of standard analytical techniques, although it did not address issues that were considered by many associated with the academic economics establishment to be central to economics at the time. Best was also a highly respected teacher.

Best's initial two-year appointment required that he be considered for reappointment during his second year in the Economics Department, 1970–1971. By then, as pointed out by the visiting committee, the Department under Kindahl's leadership was clearly moving in one of the directions, namely, economic theory, that Kindahl had earlier identified as important to the rebuilding of the Department, and that the academic establishment in economics was promoting and pursuing. One way in which the current standards of the establishment were clearly acknowledged in the Department was by the emphasis of several new hires on mathematics as a tool in analyzing economic reality. However, Best, the radical, was not following an establishment-sanctioned path, and perhaps partly because of this, his research, in relation to the goals set out by Kindahl and the criteria of the establishment, was judged by a majority of the Department's personnel committee (in its advisory capacity) to be weak and lack creativity. Early in December, Kindahl recommended a one-year terminal reappointment that would require Best to leave the University in June of 1972. It is likely that Kindahl was trying to build on, or at least not lose, the momentum in recruiting that had been created during the previous two years. By releasing faculty who did not seem to meet standards as soon as possible, space would become available for replacements more quickly. Kindahl would be able to attract high-quality replacements in part because the policy of early dismissal would help to demonstrate the considerable potential of the Department and its commitment to academic excellence.

However, Alfange, the new dean of the Faculty of Social and Behavioral Science (along with some economics faculty members), thought early dismissal to be both unusual and unfair. Customary campus practice relating to tenure-track appointees had been to provide them with a full six years before the required tenure decision in order to give them the fullest opportunity to amass a record worthy of the granting of tenure. This would certainly apply in the case of an outstanding and popular teacher like Best. Therefore, later on during the spring semester, Alfange (with the concurrence of his own dean's-level advisory personnel committee) recommended to Provost Gluckstern a two- year reappointment without prejudice of either further reappointment or termination.

Meanwhile, upon returning from winter break at the end of January, the students took up Best's cause. A vigorous protest ensued that included, in the first half of February, a number of articles and letters in the student newspaper, *The Massachusetts Daily Collegian*, castigating the University for its reappointment policies. In the end, Gluckstern chose a compromise and agreed to a one-year reappointment without prejudice of either further reappointment or termination. This meant, of course, that Best would have to come up for reappointment again in the following year.

At some time in late January or February, both Smith (who had been deeply involved in the rebuilding process) and Kindahl, came to the conclusion, rightly or wrongly, that they and their efforts to rebuild the Economics Department had lost the administrative support that they had enjoyed under Hunsberger and Shapiro. In their view, the administration had become sympathetic to the dissidents in the Department. As yet, no statement of backing for Kindahl as recommended by the visiting committee had been forthcoming. Indeed, there had been, to that point, no public comment at all from the administration on the committee's report. (A public statement to the Economics Department was made by Alfange in a memo dated March 19, 1971.) It is not clear if, at that time, Smith and Kindahl knew of Alfange's position on the Best reappointment. But if they did, this certainly would have contributed to their feelings of lost support. Moreover, they were aware of the pressure for Best's reappointment coming from the students and some faculty members and, if they had not yet heard from Alfange on the matter, it is likely that they also would have interpreted his absence of comment as further lack of support.

In an informal handwritten letter on February 2, 1971, Smith signaled to Kindahl his intent to resign from the Department as soon as he was able to decide where he would relocate. An official letter to Kindahl stating the same thing was dated March 15. Kindahl submitted his own letter of resignation from the head position (not from the Department) on February 25. Addressed to Alfange and the Economics Department, it began as follows:

> In 1968 I agreed to become Head of the Department of Economics. At that time I was convinced that the University Administration could and would provide the resources and the support necessary to build a first-rate Department. I am no longer convinced that this will be done while I am Head.

Kindahl's resignation was to be effective "… as soon as feasible … and no later than August 31, 1971." The role that these resignations had, if any, in persuading the outstanding economist mentioned in the previous quotation from the visiting committee's report to decline the Economics Department's offer is not known. However, the possibility of their significance cannot be ruled out.

It could be argued that Kindahl failed in his building efforts because, in the Amherst campus's political climate of the period, he was moving too narrowly and too quickly. He clearly held a very strong position in that he had all of the high-profile academic stars in the Department on his side at a time when the administration was committed to enhancing the academic stature of the faculty. The administration may have expected the Kindahl faction to sweep aside its opposition within the Department by the sheer force of its superior academic credentials. Indeed, the purpose of appointing the 1970 visiting review committee may have been to allow the administration to confirm its view that the Department leadership was right and that the opposition was standing in the way of the achievement of academic excellence. But by appearing to focus so heavily on the rapid creation of a group of mathematically inclined microeconomists at the expense of other important areas of the discipline, such as macroeconomics,[14] Kindahl caused the members of the review committee to caution that the opposition's case had substantial merit, a conclusion that may have taken the administration aback.

Moreover, Kindahl's unwillingness to renew Best's appointment, aroused further opposition from faculty and student quarters. The students at the time were pressing their case that the University was concerned only about research and scholarship to the exclusion of teaching, and a campus norm had developed that an outstanding teacher ought to be given the fullest chance to compile a record of scholarship that would justify the award of tenure. Granting Best reappointments for six years up to the time of normal tenure consideration would permit, should his scholarly record then warrant it, a negative decision to be safely and successfully made. However, by refusing to wait, Kindahl earned the distrust of a significant number

---

14. Kindahl's efforts (mentioned earlier) to hire monetary economists and other less-mathematically inclined personnel did not change this appearance.

of students and faculty (both inside and outside the Department) and of the administration, many of whom saw the denial of reappointment (and a second attempt to deny reappointment the following year when Kindahl was no longer head—see Chapter 6) as an ideological and political move.

Of course, it could also be contended that to be successful in building a first-rate department, one has to take quick advantage of opportunities as they arise. The availability of sought-after faculty does not occur often and the window of their availability does not usually last long. Furthermore, restricting attention to specific fields can severely limit the quality of the faculty that can be hired because good people in the required fields may not be available at the right time and better people might be available at that time in other fields. Thus, to build a top-notch department, it is often necessary to hire the best of those available and to try to resolve any field imbalances later. These kinds of considerations were likely driving Kindahl to move quickly and disregard field issues, and he no doubt thought he had the support of the administration to do so.

In any event, it is remarkable how close Kindahl came to realizing his goal of creating a first-rate Economics Department that would be recognized as such by the economics establishment. Building departments of this sort is not easy. It requires large measures of skill and luck, often over a period of many, many years. Skill is a prerequisite for recognizing and taking advantage of opportunities; luck is essential in that the appropriate opportunities have to present themselves at the right time. Had Smith not resigned and had Kindahl's success in hiring extended into the 1970–1971 academic year, the necessary foundation would have been firmly in place in the brief space of three recruiting seasons. The likelihood of achieving first-rate status shortly thereafter would have been very high since the filling of the gaps in personnel pointed out by the visiting committee would probably have been relatively easy. However, it was not to be. Instead, and equally remarkable, the Department veered off onto an unexpectedly unorthodox and unexpectedly successful course. The transition to that new course is considered next.

Chapter 6

The Transition to Radical Political Economics

Kindahl's resignation caught Dean Alfange by surprise. It came (barely) early enough for him to appoint a search committee with the charge of recommending a replacement (as either head or chair) in sufficient time to make an offer by May 1, 1971. The committee was made up of seven persons, four of whom were members of the Economics Department faculty. Now, in the wake of Kindahl's resignation, the Department was badly split between those who had favored Kindahl and his policies and those who had not. Because it was, therefore, clear that no internal faculty member would have the support of most of the Department, the committee had to look outside for a head or chair. Names of potential candidates were solicited from various sources, five were brought to the campus for interviews, one withdrew, and the committee was left to choose among four candidates. Of the four, two monetary economists had the most support: John M. Culbertson of the University of Wisconsin and Daniel Orr of the University of California at San Diego. However, the existing divisions in the Department were represented on the committee and, although the committee as a whole voted five-to-two in favor of Culbertson, the four economics faculty members were evenly divided two-to-two between Culbertson and Orr. Those supporting Orr had also sided with Kindahl in earlier disputes. The majority view, of course, prevailed and the search committee report of April 15 recommended Culbertson. However, observing the split among the economics faculty members on the committee, Alfange asked the full Department to vote on the four candidates. The result was fifteen for Culbertson and eight for Orr, with four abstentions.

In the face of this dissension, Alfange was unwilling to accept the April 15 report of the search committee. Instead, he asked the committee to look further and to try to come up with additional possibilities. Several candidates who were previously not considered were found, and two of them visited the campus. The second report of the search committee recommended Simon Rottenberg of Duke University to be the new head or chair. In this case, the vote on the committee was five-to-one in favor, one of the committee members having resigned in the interim. The subsequent Department vote recorded nine dissenting ballots, many of which had probably come from faculty members who were allied with Kindahl and who had previously backed Orr. Tensions in the Department were running high. In a letter, dated May 17, to those who had dissented from the Committee's recommendation of Rottenberg, Alfange refers to meetings with "... members of the Department that were intended as means of alleviating tensions, but which proved to have the opposite effect ...." At this point, however, Alfange accepted the committee's report and Rottenberg was appointed head of the Economics Department. Alfange believed that Rottenberg would be an effective head in spite of the tensions, and that he was the best candidate available, given the Department's needs. Alfange also hoped that Rottenberg would be able to bring a period of calm and healing to the Department.

Simon Rottenberg was a distinguished economist with publications in a variety of areas. He was considered to be a member of the Chicago School of Economics. Apart from its genesis and

Simon Rottenberg, March, 1978. *(Courtesy of Special Collections and University Archives, W.E.B. Du Bois Library, University of Massachusetts at Amherst)*

base in the University of Chicago's Economics Department, the main characteristics of adherents to that school were, according to M.W. Reder,[1] "(1) belief in the power of neoclassical price theory to explain observed economic behaviour [sic]; and (2) belief in the efficacy of free markets to allocate resources and distribute income. The latter was associated with a belief in the desirability of minimizing the role of the state in [private] economic activity."[2] Rottenberg did not employ mathematics in the building of his theoretical constructions, but his economic reasoning was nonetheless deep and sophisticated.

Rottenberg assumed the duties of head of Department on September 1, 1971, and a new recruitment effort was begun. A significant number of economists were identified and several were invited to the campus for further consideration. I was one of the

1. "Chicago School," *The New Palgrave,* v. 1, J. Eatwell, M. Milgate, and P. Newman, eds. (London: Macmillan, 1987), p. 413.
2. Rottenberg's feelings in this regard were spelled out some years later in a letter to James E. Cathey dated January 23, 1979.

latter. At the time, I was an untenured, full professor at the University of Waterloo in Ontario, Canada and was doing and had a reputation for work in mathematical microeconomics. The fact that I was given serious consideration suggests that Rottenberg had nothing against the hiring of mathematical economists and, probably, had gained acceptance and support among those who were allied with Kindahl and had initially voted against him. But no offers emerged from this recruitment effort because Rottenberg resigned from the head position before any could be made.

There were two events that played a major role in Rottenberg's resignation. First, as indicated in Chapter 4, Samuel S. Bowles, who was then a well-known associate professor at Harvard and who, after doing work that was highly regarded by the economics establishment, became a leader in the radical political economy movement (his approach to economics was described in Chapter 1), was going to be considered for tenure at Harvard during the 1972–1973 academic year. He thought tenure would be denied, was certain that there would be a bitter battle in the Harvard Economics Department over it, and wanted to be away from Harvard during that time to avoid the unpleasantness he thought likely to arise from interacting with those who were engaged in that battle. Early in the fall of 1971, Bowles contacted Best on the University of Massachusetts's Amherst campus economics faculty and told him that he (Bowles) would be receptive to a visiting appointment at the University of Massachusetts at Amherst for the following academic year. Best informed the Economics Department at a Department meeting and the matter was referred to the Department's personnel committee. The latter rejected the idea. It is likely that Rottenberg was involved in the personnel committee's discussion and concurred with its decision. There the matter might have rested were it not for a chance encounter between Best and Alfange somewhere on the

Amherst campus. Best told Alfange what had happened. The latter was elated at the possibility that an economist as visible as Bowles might be induced to spend a year at the University and approached Rottenberg with the proposal that Bowles be given a visiting position in the Economics Department for 1972–1973. This time, Rottenberg consulted with colleagues outside of the Department for whom he had considerable respect (including an editor of the *American Economic Review*) and with the Department's personnel committee. The answer that came back to Alfange was negative. Rottenberg believed that Bowles "... was very bright and charming and technically competent, that his earlier work had been promising, but that he no longer did serious scientific work."[3] Alfange, who had consulted with a different group of prominent economists (including three future Nobel laureates) and had received glowing reports of Bowles's work and promise from them, thought that Rottenberg's refusal was ideologically and politically motivated and not based on academic standards.[4] In spite of this, Alfange was unwilling to force Bowles's appointment on an objecting Department. At that point, Harvey L. Friedman, who was then the director of the University's Labor Relations and Research Center and who had heard of what was going on from Best, offered to give Bowles a visiting faculty appointment in his Center. This was not unappealing to Bowles due, in part, to the close intellectual ties between radical economists and the labor movement. Consequently, Bowles spent the 1972–1973 academic year as a visiting professor in the Labor Center.

3. Rottenberg, S., "Response to Dean Alfange," *Measure*, September, 1974: 4.
4. The views of Rottenberg and Alfange on this, the (second) reappointment of Best, and the hiring of the radical package (both of which will be considered momentarily) are clearly expressed in exchanges between them that appeared in the May 1974 (pp. 3, 5) and September 1974 (pp. 3–5) issues of *Measure*, a publication of the University Centers for Rational Alternatives.

Samuel S. Bowles, February, 1977. (*Courtesy of Special Collections and University Archives, W.E.B. Du Bois Library, University of Massachusetts at Amherst*)

It is not hard to understand where Rottenberg was coming from. His adherence to the Chicago School has already been noted.[5] Given that as the basis for his approach to economics, it is natural to expect that Rottenberg would believe that Bowles's then-current work did not fall in the realm of what he (Rottenberg) considered to be (scientific) economics and did not, therefore, meet current professional standards. Alfange, on the other hand, had the support of the administration and genuinely believed that the radical challenge to the dominant establishment orthodoxy was intellectually viable and significant, and ought to be represented in the Department. This divergence of views also mirrored, although not as unequally, the lopsided split in the economics profession at the time previously described in Chapter 4. The large majority of economists and the economics establishment would have

5. It is ironic that the Economics Department at the University of Chicago had shown interest in adding Bowles to its faculty on two previous occasions—first as a new PhD and second when he was fired from Harvard for not signing the loyalty oath required by Massachusetts law (recall Chapter 4).

shared Rottenberg's view, whereas the small minority would have backed Alfange and the administration. The two men were unable to bridge this gap, distrust grew between them, and each was seen by the other as lacking credibility with respect to administrative judgments.

The unfortunate development of distrust was important in the second event that led directly to Rottenberg's resignation. Working now in the field of radical political economy, Best, who had been given only a one-year reappointment the previous year, was again up for reappointment. Again he received strong support from the students. This time the Department's personnel committee unanimously advised against reappointment. Rottenberg's own evaluation of the case then led to a recommendation from him of nonrenewal (perhaps for reasons similar to those on the basis of which he had rejected a visiting position for Bowles). However, the personnel committee of the Faculty of Social and Behavioral Sciences (which makes advisory recommendations to the dean on all personnel actions relating to faculty in the College) voted to override Rottenberg's recommendation and favor renewal. Rottenberg then asked for, and was granted an opportunity to meet with the College personnel committee to present his case. During that meeting, he persuaded enough committee members to change their minds so that the committee vote now concurred with his recommendation. However, a committee member who was unable to attend that meeting demurred, demanding a third vote—this time of the full committee. Meanwhile, student activity in support of Best heated up and culminated in a meeting between two protesting students and Randolph Bromery who was then chancellor of the Amherst campus. In the end, with Alfange and the administration distrusting Rottenberg and believing that the Department's decision was

Norman D. Aitken, November, 1998. *(Courtesy of Special Collections and University Archives, W.E.B. Du Bois Library, University of Massachusetts at Amherst)*

ideologically and politically motivated and unfair, it was reversed. Best was reappointed for a period of three years, long enough to take him through his tenure-decision year. Rottenberg immediately resigned the head position, remaining in the Department as a faculty member. The split and high tensions in the Department that Alfange had hoped Rottenberg would heal were, respectively, as wide and acute as ever.

Needing a head or chair for the Economics Department, and having no possibilities acceptable to a reasonable percentage of economics faculty in sight, Provost Gluckstern appointed Alfange as acting head of the Department in July. The latter responsibilities were in addition to his obligations as dean of the Faculty of Social and Behavioral Sciences. Alfange, in turn, appointed Norman D. Aitken, a tenured assistant professor in the Department who had just spent the previous academic year on leave in England doing research at the London School of Economics Library, as administrative officer to handle the day-to-day operations of departmental administration.[6]

Alfange (before he was appointed acting head of the Economics Department) and Bowles had a number of discussions that spring, mostly relating to the Economics Department's refusal to offer Bowles a visiting appointment. Somewhere along the way, Bowles suggested to Alfange that, if, as anticipated, he were denied tenure at Harvard, he might be interested in a permanent move to the Economics Department at the University of Massachusetts in Amherst provided that some sort of package of radical economists could be put together.[7] Informal discussions continued during the summer. The two even met on a chicken farm on Mt. Desert island in Maine where Alfange happened to be while Bowles was living for a month in return for working in a local shipyard doing maintenance and repair on the chicken-farm owner's boat.[8]

September came and Bowles took up his visiting position at the Labor Center. University policy required every department to vote at the start of the semester on the constitution of a personnel committee to deal with hiring and other personnel matters during the coming academic year. At this point, and with no abatement of tensions over the summer, the Economics Department voted to have no personnel committee. The Department was so deeply and evenly divided that each side probably feared that the other would capture

6. Aitken joined the Department as an instructor in the fall of 1964 and became an assistant professor upon completion of his PhD degree at the University of Tennessee in 1967. On the basis of one paper published in the *American Economic Review* and one of publishable quality later appearing in the same journal, Kindahl recommended and Aitken was granted tenure in 1970, although he remained at the assistant professor level. Aitken was not promoted to the associate level until 1976, one year after he had left the chair position in the Economics Department to which he was appointed (as indicated later) in 1973.

7. The phrase *radical package* was coined by Kindahl later on.

8. As Bowles put it, this was just post the 1960s and one did not have to be too weird to do things like that.

the committee and make decisions hostile to its interests. However, the effect of that vote was to give Alfange a totally free hand in all personnel matters. And the opportunity for action was considerable. The University was still growing by 100 new faculty positions each year, many of which were allocated to the Faculty of Social and Behavioral Sciences to be distributed by Alfange, the dean. With this as background, Alfange informed Department members of the procedures he would follow as acting Department head on hiring and other personnel actions in a memo dated September 26, 1972.

As expected, Bowles was denied tenure by the Economics Department at Harvard that fall. Alfange immediately raised the possibility with him of a tenured appointment in the Economics Department of the University of Massachusetts at Amherst. But Bowles was reluctant because he had witnessed other radical economists, who had taken appointments as token representatives of their approach in other departments, become isolated and marginalized. If Bowles were to accept, it would have to be, as he had suggested to Alfange earlier, as part of a package of perhaps five radical economists. Due to substantial allocations of faculty positions in other departments in Social and Behavioral Sciences during preceding years, none had significant need for new appointments. Alfange was thus free to assign to Economics enough of the new positions he had been given for the 1972–1973 academic year to make such a package possible.[9] Thus, he agreed to recommend the idea of a package provided that Bowles could identify four additional radical scholars of recognized stature who would be willing to move to Amherst.

Bowles set out to do just that. Two persons at Harvard, Richard C. Edwards (a recent graduate student there) and Herbert Gintis

---

9. As it turned out, and as will be noted later, Alfange actually made a total number of eleven offers that year. Not all, but more than just the five in the radical package, were accepted.

Richard C. Edwards, August, 1984. *(Courtesy of Special Collections and University Archives, W.E.B. Du Bois Library, University of Massachusetts at Amherst)*

(a graduate student at Harvard and then an assistant professor there[10]) were obvious choices. Bowles had worked closely with both of them and had very high opinions of each. Bowles also called Steven A. Resnick (an associate professor) and Richard D. Wolff (an assistant professor), both at City College in New York, whom he knew less well but respected enormously. Although Wolff had been a graduate student at Yale while Resnick was an assistant professor there, the two did not meet until Resnick moved to City College in 1971. Thereafter they came to know each other well because

10. Gintis began graduate school as a student in the Mathematics Department at Harvard University in 1961. But the political turmoil of the 1960s described, in part, in Chapter 3, had a profound affect on him. Around the time of President John F. Kennedy's assassination in November of 1963, Gintis decided that "... mathematics was not sufficiently in tune with the events of... [the] times," and switched to economics. Although never having taken an economics course, "... a friend who had studied Marx [had] told... [him that economics] was a good field because 'economics determines everything else.'" (P. Arestis and M. Sawyer, eds., *A Biographical Dictionary of Dissenting Economists*, 2nd ed. [Cheltenham: Elgar, 2000], p. 226.)

Herbert Gintis, January, 1977. (*Courtesy of Special Collections and University Archives, W.E.B. Du Bois Library, University of Massachusetts at Amherst*)

they regularly commuted by train together between their homes in the New Haven area and New York City. All four were interested in Bowles's proposal. That winter they arranged to meet as a group with Bowles at his home in Ashfield, Massachusetts to discuss the possibility of jointly moving to Amherst.

The meeting was a great success. In addition to becoming better acquainted with each other and with the differences in their approaches to radical political economy (precursors of what was described in Chapter 1), there were discussions about the kinds of research that would be undertaken in Amherst, the nature of courses that would be taught, and the structure of a graduate program in radical political economy. The idea of a radical group of this size in the Amherst-campus Economics Department was attractive for a number of reasons: (1) The University of Massachusetts was a state school and was, therefore, more identified with the middle- and lower-income classes—populations with which the radical econo-mists wanted to interact. (2) The radicals would no longer be lone

Steven A. Resnick (standing) and Richard D. Wolff (seated), November, 1990. *(Courtesy of Special Collections and University Archives, W.E.B. Du Bois Library, University of Massachusetts at Amherst)*

and isolated aliens in a traditional department. They would have positions of power and could read and explore Marxism and other parts of radical political economy as they wished. (3) It would be much easier to teach Marxism under such conditions than at more traditional departments where courses in that subject often met with considerable faculty resistance and, when they were offered, sometimes had to be taught in excess of standard teaching loads. And (4) there would be a unique, heterogeneous graduate program in radical political economy (heterogeneous due to the differences in approaches among them) that would be unlikely to exist in the same form elsewhere. All agreed that they would commit to joining the University of Massachusetts' Economics Department only as a group—all or nothing—and, should the offers be forthcoming, remain there for at least five years. This was the radical package that was presented to Alfange. Bowles and Resnick were to be tenured at full rank. Gintis and Wolff would have tenure at the associate rank.[11] Edwards, essentially a new PhD at the time, would be an assistant professor on a tenure track with a three-year appointment.

Subsequently, Edwards, Gintis, Resnick, and Wolff visited the Amherst campus. (Bowles was already on campus at the University's Labor Center.) Given what had recently transpired in the Department, it is not surprising that there was opposition to the hiring of the radical package. The same reasons for denying Bowles a visiting appointment and Best reappointment, resentment that Alfange, a political scientist, was following through without regard to what they considered to be the standards of the economics profession, and the feeling that Alfange had usurped the rights and powers of the Department, fueled the opposition. However, in a memo to the Department dated February 26, 1973, Alfange argued that he had acted appropriately. The Department had ceded all power over personnel matters to him. Although he had requested faculty input along the way, he did not receive it from all quarters. He regarded the opposition as politically motivated. Moreover, Alfange was, by these appointments, hoping for a large "... increase in undergraduate interest in economics ..."—an interest that, at that time, was not commensurate with the size of the economics faculty. He thought of these appointments as an unusual opportunity to give the Department considerable strength, visibility, and diversity.[12] And he

11. Tenure for Wolff raised a special problem. According to University of Massachusetts standards at the time, he had not been out of graduate school long enough for tenure to be granted. However, since he had just been approved for tenure at City College and, therefore, would have been in a tenured position had he remained there, Wolff indicated that he was unwilling to move to Amherst without it. The University's tenure rules did not appear to cover such a situation but, in any case, Wolff's tenure was approved.

12. Recall that one of the recommendations of the visiting review committee's report of 1971 was that new appointments to the Department should add diversity. In addition to their radical perspectives, individuals in the radical package represented the fields of economic development, economic history, industrial organization, and the economics of education.

was supported in this venture by several well-known and prominent economists outside the Department, in addition to those originally supporting the Bowles visiting appointment as described earlier.

Remember that this was a time of activism on campus stemming from the anti-Vietnam-War movement. As described earlier, the students had already protested on each occasion the two separate attempts in two successive years by the Economics Department to terminate the radical Best. The attitude of the University administration during this period (as suggested in Chapter 3) was seen as being sensitive to student concerns and willing to take them into account whenever it was possible and reasonable to do so. Because the radicals in the package were all known as excellent and even, in some cases, inspiring teachers and scholars, because the administration wanted, as previously indicated, to pique student curiosity in economics, because student interests during that period often tended to be oriented toward issues on the left, and because, apart from the classroom, the radicals were sympathetic to, if not at that time, fully engaged in the antiwar movement, the hiring of the radical package could, therefore, be seen as providing the additional benefit that it offered evidence of the administration's willingness to heed student views.

Provost Gluckstern and Chancellor Tippo had some reservations about the ramifications of hiring so many radical economists. However, their reluctance faded in the face of the outside support referred to earlier, the implied enhancement of the academic standing of the Economics Department, and the all-or-nothing ultimatum presented by the radicals. Moreover, they had concluded (as previously mentioned) that the refusal of the Department to give Bowles a visiting appointment, despite the strong endorsements he had received from some of the nation's most outstanding economists, was based on ideological and political, rather than academic, criteria. But whereas offers of appointment are bestowed by the provost, only the University's trustees can grant tenure. And without tenure for all four radicals appointed at the associate and full professor ranks, the deal that would bring the radical package to the University would collapse. Once again, it was additional support from the same group of highly visible economists outside of the University that made the difference, and tenure was awarded to all four. Thus, in Alfange's words,[13]

> The radical package had become a reality—somewhat to the surprise of at least some members of the package who expected that the proposal to hire them would be derailed by conservatives. The latter, they thought, would make a public issue of the fact that a state university was planning to appoint a large group of economists who took the ideas of Karl Marx seriously, and would put pressure on the legislature and the Trustees to prevent that from occurring. That could easily have been done. Why it was not done, I do not know. I only know that throughout the entire process, I received no warnings of public disapproval. I did get a call from a reporter for the *Boston Globe* who had heard of the proposal to hire Marxist economists. I told him that it would be helpful if the issue were not prominently publicized. He said he recognized that. All that subsequently appeared in the *Globe* was a brief innocuous and noninflamatory item on an inside page.

There is some irony here in that Kindahl was defeated in his attempt to build a significant Economics Department (Chapter 5) by forces favoring intradepartmental democracy whereas Alfange, who also

---

13. As recorded in a document attached to a letter dated August 4, 2003, and edited by me. Reproduced with permission.

believed in that democracy, succeeded by acting as a nondemo-
cratic head.

Alfange's motivations in hiring the radical package were set out
in a memorandum to the members of the Economics Department
dated February 26, 1973. He apparently was aware that the radicals
had many detractors among prestigious members of the economics
profession. However, as previously noted, he had also been told by
other prestigious members how highly qualified as economists the
radicals were. Alfange regarded their appointment as "... an unpar-
alleled opportunity... to make a major step forward in terms of the
professional excellence of the department." He also thought that "...
the department needed to be broadened... in order to reflect more
widely the professional views that... [were] held in the discipline at
[the time]." Moreover, in light of the specific fields within economics that the radicals represented (e.g., economic development, economic history, industrial organization, and the economics of education), the appointment of the radical package would be "... a means
of redressing the imbalance of the past" as identified in the visiting
review committee report of January, 1971.

Alfange also made a number of other offers of positions in the
Economics Department to individuals he saw as nonradical economists who were intended to counterbalance the radical appointments. Several of those were accepted. In addition to three assistant
professors, a visiting full-professor appointment for fall of 1973 was
agreed to by Leonard A. Rapping. At that time, Rapping was a professor of economics at Carnegie-Mellon University. He was known,
in part, for his work with Robert E. Lucas, Jr. (a future Nobel laureate) on the macroeconomics of employment, wages, and inflation.
Although nothing ever came of it, Kindahl and the Department
Personnel Committee had considered Rapping for an appointment to the Department in the fall of 1970. But Rapping had been

radicalized by the Vietnam War and his approach to economics had shifted accordingly. This fact was probably not known to either Kindahl or Alfange.[14]

At the same time, many of those who had sided with Kindahl were looking for positions at other universities. Smith had already left, although his official resignation would come later. Sonnenschein had accepted an appointment elsewhere. The latter had decided to leave before the hiring of the radical package became a significant possibility because, like Smith, he thought that the Department had lost the support of the administration in its efforts to build a significant faculty The exodus continued for several more years.

Shortly after he became acting head, Alfange appointed a search committee to find a permanent head or chair of the Department. On January 25, the Department met to consider the committee's recommendation to appoint Aitken, the Department's administrative officer, to that position. The vote was eleven in favor, eight against, and three abstentions. The committee did not think that this support was strong enough to bring its recommendation of Aitken to the dean. So the committee continued its work, and, on April 11, 1973, it voted to recommend Rapping, who was already on board as a visiting professor for the following fall, as Department head. Along with the head position, Rapping would be given a full professorship with tenure. At a Department meeting on April 19, a vote was taken in which thirteen supported the recommendation, one voted against it, and there were four abstentions. Subsequently two faculty members who did not attend the meeting voiced their support. An undated second report by the head of the search committee to the Department, in which Rapping is recommended, suggests

14. One of the assistant professors in this group of new recruits was also listed as a radical in the Department's classification scheme developed later on.

that the committee thought of Rapping as a nonradical economist who could bridge the gap between the radicals and the remainder of the Department. Apparently they had not realized that Rapping had recently become a radical himself. However, in a memorandum dated May 24, 1973, Rapping indicated that, after first accepting it, he was declining the offer as Department head because, upon further reflection, he felt that he was not up to the job. Rapping, moreover, asked if he could still accept the tenured, full-professor part of the offer. That request was granted and Rapping moved to Amherst in time for the start of the fall 1973 semester.

At this point the search committee went back to its earlier recommendation of Aitken, who was then installed as Department chair (not head). Aitken faced a daunting task. Animosity and distrust abounded in the Department. There was also the fear that, upon their arrival, the radicals would impose their own brand of orthodoxy (as, some believed, the neoclassical economists had when Kindahl was head), isolating and marginalizing certain nonradical faculty.

Chapter 7

The First Three Years of
Radical Presence

At the end of the 1972–1973 academic year, Bowles returned to Harvard. He did not take up his position in the Economics Department of the University of Massachusetts until the fall of 1974 when Gintis accompanied him. However, Edwards, Resnick, Wolff, and Rapping all arrived for the fall 1973 semester. By then, a handful of radical students had also entered the graduate PhD program in economics. During the previous year's recruiting process that led to the hiring of the radical package, word had got out among the students at City College in New York that there might be a significant contingent of radical economists joining the Amherst campus's Economics Department in the near future. This was especially attractive to a number of students who had studied Marxism under Resnick and Wolff and had become very interested in it. Desiring advanced degrees in economics, these students applied and were accepted to several economics graduate programs including that at the University of Massachusetts. When it became clear that the economists in the radical package were actually moving to Amherst, this group of students decided to go with them.

However, in the fall of 1973, the Economics Department was in turmoil. Smith and Sonnenschein were gone. Others had left or were in the process of leaving. Among those who remained, there was a sizable group who had opposed the hiring of the radical package and were unhappy even with its partial presence. Simmering in the background were all the tensions and hurt feelings that had been brought on by battles over the previous four years. Somehow, in this environment, the radicals had to be integrated into the Department, the PhD program (there was no MA program of any consequence) had to be revised to accommodate the interests of the new radical faculty members and the new radical graduate students and, at the undergraduate level, major courses and service courses for noneconomics majors from other departments had to be maintained so as to continue to meet outside expectations. It was a daunting task that would involve more faculty departures and more battles, and would take several more years. Moreover, there was no precedent in anyone's knowledge for achieving a balanced department with respect to such diverse and controversial paradigms of economic thought as were now represented in the Department. Nor was anyone aware of how to structure a graduate program that would be consistent with that balance. The process of balancing, if that was to be attempted, was necessarily one of trial and error, and of working through multiple and conflicting concerns.

There were also matters that the radical faculty had to face by themselves. For the first time in their professional lives they were able to pursue their radicalism full time, in any way they chose, and without hindrance and outside pressure distracting them or pushing them in more traditional directions. How was this to be done? What topics should be considered and what problems should they attempt to solve? What methods should be employed? There were also questions relating to teaching: What should be taught? How should it be taught? What should be the relation, if any, between the various courses in radical economics and between radical and nonradical courses? And, of course, there were matters relating to intradepartmental politics: what to do with the new power the radicals had, what strategies and tactics to use, and so forth. The answers to these and other questions had to be worked out and the absence of precedent, the necessity of trial and error, and the resolution of multiple and conflicting concerns applied here as well. The Departmental PhD program that emerged from these discussions and interactions was a program intensely focused on radical political economy that emphasized the alternative paradigmatic approaches to economics set out in Chapter 1 (neoclassical, Marxism combined with political and social liberalism, Marxism combined with Keynesian macroeconomics, and mutual interaction of all analytical elements). The neoclassical paradigm was represented in a limited way. Only the very fundamental concepts and relations were included. The idea was for the paradigm to serve as a basis for the criticism of neoclassical thought in general and to be available for comparison to the radical political economy paradigms in particular. In addition to certain basic course requirements, two written comprehensive examinations chosen from theoretical fields linked to different paradigms or combinations of paradigms were required. No traditional program of study, like that available at other universities, was offered.

The atmosphere in the radical camp has been described by James R. Crotty, who actually joined the Department a year later and of whose arrival more will be said later. Although Crotty was writing about the period starting with the fall of 1974, his words apply in spirit to the 1973–1974 academic year as well:[1]

It was an extremely intellectually exciting first few years. At that time, none of us had what we thought to be a mature, fully articulated theory of radical political economy. Bowles and Gintis were

1. From a document attached to e-mail correspondence dated June 8, 2006, as edited by me. Reproduced here with permission.

often in transition. Resnick and Wolff arrived in Amherst as traditional Hegelian Marxists but began to shift towards their mutually-constitutive-interaction approach shortly thereafter. Rapping changed his mind weekly. The point is that we were all talking with each other, looking to learn from each other, and all of us were open to change to some degree. Rapping was an incredibly creative thinker, always searching for new ways of approaching economics. He and I had a huge number of wonderfully stimulating conversations about every aspect of economic theory imaginable, and never went over the same material twice. We all felt we were taking part in a common project of great importance—the creation of a new and significant body of knowledge and the first, first-rate radical-political-economy graduate program—things for which we had no blueprint.

The publications that eventually resulted from these activities and interactions were numerous. For example, Bowles and Gintis began to explore

... the difficulties of grounding democratic theory [solely] on either liberalism (due to its tendency to overlook power relations in the economy and the family, and its pre-social concept of the individual endowed with exogenously given wants and capacities) or Marxism (due to its tendency to underrate the despotic potential of the state, and its underdeveloped theory of individual choice)....
[Drawing on both sources, they ultimately developed a foundation] for democratic theory based on a political conception of markets and economic organization and a model of individual action and human development in which both choice and social influences on individual development were given prominence.[2]

2. P. Arestis and M. Sawyer, eds., *A Biographical Dictionary of Dissenting Economists*, 2nd ed. (Cheltenham: Elgar, 2000), p. 77.

This was published as S. Bowles and H. Gintis, *Democracy and Capitalism: Property, Community, and the Contradictions of Modern Social Thought* (New York: Basic books, 1986). The book "... may be considered a critique of the capitalist economy and an argument for the radical potential of democratic (rather than specifically socialist) demands in a capitalist society."[3]

At the same time Resnick and Wolff were starting to work out the philosophical and methodological details of their mutually interactive approach to Marxian analysis described in Chapter 1. All forms of economic determinism were rejected, and they eventually applied their approach to obtain a new understanding of the economic firm and a new interpretation of the state in market economies. Their concept of economic class (p. 14) lay at the core of this analysis. In particular, they developed a theory of class and used it to probe the class structure of both the firm and the state. The end result was S.A. Resnick and R.D. Wolff, *Knowledge and Class: A Marxian Critique of Political Economy* (Chicago: University of Chicago Press, 1987).

As a third example of the creativity that emerged from the stimulating environment within the University of Massachusetts at Amherst Economics Department at the time, consider that the year 1974 was one of turmoil in the United States. Richard M. Nixon had resigned the U.S. Presidency on August 9 and the U.S. economy was experiencing significant inflation along with the high unemployment that accompanies recession. It was not so long before that that most economists believed that this simultaneous occurrence of unemployment and inflation was not possible (see Chapter 4). The 1975 Economic Report of the President's Council of Economic Advisers was issued over the signature of its chairman,

3. Ibid.

Alan Greenspan, in January of 1975. That report, reflecting the understandings of the economics establishment, attributed the economic difficulties of 1974 to government policy errors and the OPEC oil embargo. Crotty and Rapping disagreed. In J.R. Crotty and L.A. Rapping, "The 1975 Report of the President's Council of Economic Advisers: A Radical Critique," *American Economic Review* 65 (1975), pp. 791–811, they argued, contrary to the establishment view, that the 1974 economic situation, which they referred to as a "crisis," was "... systemic in nature and that the [expansionary] macropolicies of the... [previous] decade were rational and perhaps unavoidable given the political-economic objectives [in part to support the war in Vietnam] and [the] constraints facing the macropolicy authorities" (p. 791).

In addition, there was also considerable intellectual activity among other radical faculty in the Department not mentioned in Crotty's description on pp. 127–128 above, and interaction among radical economics faculty and university faculty outside of the Economics Department. These activities and interactions, along with the activities and interactions described by Crotty, extended well beyond the initial three-year period under consideration in this chapter and, with respect to the omitted activities and interactions, involved new radical hires as they joined the Department. The published output of this other group of faculty members over the extended period included important work on gender economics,[4]

---

4. *For example*, J. Humphries, "Class Struggle and the Persistence of the Working-Class Family," *Cambridge Journal of Economics* 1 (1977), pp. 241–258. Humphries joined the Economics Department in the Fall of 1973.

During this period, gender economics was concerned mostly with the characteristics of work performed by women—unpaid or domestic work not counted as part of national income, and paid work from the sale of labor time which was (and is) included in the calculation of national income—and the comparison of the latter to paid work performed by men. The comparison encompassed the analysis of wage disparities that arose when similar or identical paid work is done by a woman instead of a man.

Latin American development,[5] and the interplay between politics and economics in American capitalism.[6]

The radical graduate students had their own issues to deal with. Although there was considerable diversity of opinion among them, many were unhappy with the manner in which higher education was administered. They rebelled against the hierarchy involved and the authority that faculty had over students. In particular, they did not like the subservient relationship that graduate students often had with their mentors. They wanted more choice and flexibility in the courses and examinations that could be put together to build a degree program. They thought that more options for academic recovery should be available if a student failed a comprehensive examination. They passionately believed in the principle that all graduate students should be funded. Partly to achieve these goals, they wanted a greater degree of communication and equity in their relations with the faculty and, as described in Chapter 1, to participate in the making of departmental decisions relating to these and other matters they thought relevant to their lives as graduate students. As a consequence, activism among the graduate students directed toward the achievement of these ends became commonplace within the Department. Indeed, graduate student participation in activism was enhanced when a large group of radical graduate students (much larger than that which arrived in the

5. For example, C.D. Deere, *Household and Class Relations: Peasants and Landlords in Northern Peru* (Berkeley: University of California Press, 1990). Deere joined the Economics Department in the Fall of 1977.

6. M.H. Best and W.E. Connolly, *The Politicized Economy* (Lexington: D.C. Heath, 1976). At the time, Connolly was a faculty member of the University's Political Science Department. The book cited was based on the idea that thoughts and action interact, each potentially inducing change in the other. This approach to the analysis of real phenomenon, although overlapping with the Resnick-Wolff mutually interactive paradigm, is distinct from, and lies substantially outside of the four paradigms described in Chapter 1. Although never a part of the cross-paradigmatic debate within the Economics Department, it could be thought of as a separate paradigm on its own.

fall of 1973) was admitted to the graduate program for fall 1974, many of whom were older and were experienced activists. Be that as it may, one of the main vehicles for graduate student activism at that time was the creation during the 1973–1974 academic year of a formal organization to present, on issues deemed relevant by the graduate students, a unified "graduate student view" to the economics faculty. Called the Economics Graduate Student Organization (EGSO), this organization has played a significant role in Departmental activities and politics ever since.

Before delving into the specifics of these and other events that occurred in the early radical years, two additional matters need to be addressed. The first is the fact that for many years after 1973, practically all graduate students admitted to the Economics Department's PhD program were radical to one degree or another. There was no conscious Departmental effort to turn down nonradical applicants. It was a matter of self-selection. Department policy was to admit the most highly qualified applicants regardless of ideology and politics. Because the University of Massachusetts at Amherst had, at that time, the largest and most visible group in the country of radical economists on its faculty, because its PhD program was unique in its single-minded and intense focus on radical political economics, and because, at the University, one could, therefore, study radical political economy to an extent and depth not possible at other institutions, the University's Economics Department became the top choice among potential graduate students whose primary interests lay in this field. It turned out that these students were, on the basis of generally recognized admission credentials, highly qualified. Many had been accepted for study in graduate programs at the best universities in the country. Thus the quality of the graduate students admitted to the Department was comparable to those admitted to schools like Harvard, Chicago, Princeton, and such. The most highly qualified individuals interested in studying more traditional economics would also be accepted at those better schools and would not, because its strength now lay elsewhere, apply to the University of Massachusetts. Those originally wanting to study traditional economics who did apply to the University of Massachusetts' Amherst Economics Department, and who were prepared to accept the comparative paradigmatic program offered, did not have nearly the qualifications of the radical applicants and could not, therefore, compete with them for space in the graduate program. Many of the students entering the Department's graduate program between 1973 and 1981 (and not necessarily completing the requirements for a degree) went on to have highly successful careers inside or outside of academia. A listing of a few of the more visible names would include Michael Albert, Jack L. Amariglio, Stephen E. Cullenberg, Nancy R. Folbre, Manuel Pastor, James B. Rebitzer, David F. Ruccio, and Juliet B. Schor.

The second matter relates to the arrival of Leonard A. Rapping in the Department in the fall of 1973. Rapping's intellectual metamorphosis is rather interesting. He earned his PhD degree from the University of Chicago and, into the mid-1970s, held a position as professor of economics at Carnegie-Mellon University. He began his career as a relatively conservative economist[7] of the Chicago School. Part of his early work was an analysis of U.S. unemployment and wages between 1929 and 1958. The latter was done jointly with Robert E. Lucas, Jr., the future Nobel laureate who had an enormous impact on the economics profession. While at Carnegie-Mellon, Rapping, like others who turned to radicalism, was, as previously suggested, deeply affected by the Vietnam War,

---

7. Opinions differ about where to place Rapping on the political/ideological spectrum. The use of the phrase *relatively conservative* to describe him during his early years reflects that ambiguity. It merely suggests that before his radical conversion, Rapping was more conservative than most radical political economists.

Leonard A. Rapping, Circa 1978. *(Courtesy of Special Collections and University Archives, W.E.B. Du Bois Library, University of Massachusetts at Amherst)*

and came to believe that his approach to economics did not help in understanding what was happening in the real economic world. This led him to look around for concepts and perspectives that might provide better explanations. Though hardly a Marxist (in contrast to most other radicals at the time), Rapping was drawn to a number of radical political-economic notions that included a focus on the unemployed, class conflict, and imperialism. It was during this latter period that he was attracted to the idea of the radical package that was being put together in the Department of Economics at the University of Massachusetts. As indicated, Rapping joined the Department in the fall of 1973 (recall that he was offered the position of chair of the Department, but after initially accepting it, he subsequently declined), and in those early years he was considered to be a part of the Department's radical wing.[8]

8. It should be noted that by the mid-1980s, Rapping had become disillusioned with radical political economy and had moved back in the direction of his original political-ideological stance. See immediately preceding note 7.

During his last two years at Carnegie-Mellon (after his radical conversion) Rapping supervised the second dissertation undertaken by Crotty (recall Chapter 4) who was finishing his graduate work there while, in the first of these two years, teaching at the State University of New York at Buffalo and who, by this time, had become committed to the radical approach. As indicated earlier, the two men spent many hours together talking about economics, and these discussions continued after Crotty had moved to Bucknell University to teach there for the second year. One of the first things Rapping did upon his arrival in Amherst was to persuade the Department and administration to offer Crotty a position in the Economics Department. Although the provost at Bucknell had promised to support tenure at that university for Crotty the following year, the lure of the radical faculty and graduate students at the University of Massachusetts was too strong for him to resist. And

James R. Crotty, March 1980. *(Courtesy of Special Collections and University Archives, W.E.B. Du Bois Library, University of Massachusetts at Amherst)*

so, in the fall of 1974, Crotty became an (untenured) assistant professor of Economics on the University of Massachusetts Amherst campus.

In his first year in the Department, Crotty was a member of the graduate committee, which was responsible for all matters relating to the graduate program and graduate students. Rapping and Marshall C. Howard were also on the committee. Howard, it should be remembered, was a nonradical full professor who had served one year as acting head of the Department in the period before Kindahl assumed the head position. At some point during the 1974–1975 academic year, Jack L. Amariglio, the graduate-student chair of EGSO at the time, came to the graduate committee to complain about the method of assigning graduate-student teaching assistants to courses and faculty members. Such assignments had always been made by the Department, and the complaint was that the existing system of allocation favored some students over others. That is, semester after semester, the same students received the "good" assignments with "good" instructors from whom they could learn, whereas the remaining students appeared to be relegated to the "weaker" assignments and instructors from whom little was learned. The complaint seemed valid to the graduate committee. Amariglio proposed a new system of allocation by lottery that would be administered by EGSO with each assignment subject to the veto of the faculty member to whom the assignment was made. The committee unanimously agreed that the lottery proposal was worth trying. It was adopted by the full economics faculty on a trial basis, instituted the following semester, and has remained in place ever since. Thus, one small aspect of the graduate-students' efforts to be involved in departmental decision making had been achieved. They had become responsible for the assignment of teaching assistants.

Jack Amariglio, fall 1978. *(Courtesy of Jack Amariglio)*

Graduate student activity during the period (with particular reference to that relating to teaching assistant assignments) as seen from the perspective of the radical graduate students has been described by Amariglio:[9]

We were always meeting in those first years with the faculty. We pressured them to meet with us and we got the meetings. With regard to the allocation of teaching assistants, we told them we did not like the way things were handled. We did not like the fact that there was favoritism involved. That some people were therefore denied the opportunity to teach, which is an important skill that may be needed later. We wanted the right to make the decisions, and we wanted everybody to have the right to teach and be funded. We were constantly meeting among ourselves to discuss the politics of these and other matters—as much as two or three times a week.

9. Edited from a conversation with me on June 15, 2006. Reproduced with permission.

Thus, the first three years of radical presence in the Economics Department were marked by what was, at least from a radical perspective, considerable progress. Research programs in the three radical paradigms described in Chapter 1 were developed and beginning to be explored. A unique radical graduate program leading to the PhD degree was set up. (The specific discussions relating to the inclusion in a limited way of the neoclassical paradigm as one of the alternative paradigms in that program will be described subsequently.) A unique role for the graduate students in departmental administration was granted with respect to the allocation of teaching assistants to courses and faculty. All this was accompanied by the intense intellectual interaction and debate that characterizes the near perfection within a university community described in Chapter 1. The nonradical faculty, however, were not yet participants in that near perfection.

Nevertheless, in spite of or maybe partly because of what the radicals referred to as progress, the tensions in the Department that had now been festering and occasionally surfacing over many years once again came to the fore during 1974–1975 academic year. Granting to EGSO the responsibility for assigning teaching assistants to courses and faculty may have caused some unhappiness among the nonradical faculty, but if so, that unhappiness played only a minor role. The main explosion occurred over personnel actions. In the fall of 1974, assistant professors Michael H. Best, Che S. Tsao, and Arthur W. Wright were scheduled to be considered for tenure and promotion to associate professor. Best, as previously indicated, was radical; Tsao and Wright were not. The Department personnel committee consisted of the entire economics faculty, but, according to Department rules at the time, each person up for tenure could decide if he wanted the entire economics faculty or only the tenured economics faculty to participate in his tenure decision. Either way, the relevant

committee, which made the first recommendation to the administration on these cases, had substantial numbers of radical members.
And the academic standards for promotion and tenure adhered to by
radicals were to some extent different from the standards subscribed
to by nonradicals, not only because their view of what was mean-
ingful and significant in economics was different, but also because
they believed that teaching was a component of considerably greater
importance. Because, on the basis of those standards, the radicals all
voted in favor of tenure and promotion for Best and against tenure
and promotion for both Tsao and Wright, the votes of the personnel
committee (in its relevant form) were strongly positive for Best and
so weakly positive for Tsao and Wright (that is, there were enough
negative votes) that the granting of tenure to the latter two by the
administration was problematic. Some nonradical economics faculty
members, with their different standards for tenure and promotion,
thought these negative votes to be politically motivated. In particular,
such a conviction prompted Vaclav Holesovsky, a nonradical faculty
member in the Department who had struggled against Communism
as a Czechoslovakian citizen in Eastern Europe, to complain in a
letter to the New York Times (February 23, 1975) that the negative
votes on the personnel committee were exactly that:

> The experience in the Department of Economics of the University
> of Massachusetts at Amherst, where radical economists occupy a
> commanding position among tenured faculty and in decision-
> making bodies, has shown that they are ruthless in pursuing the
> goal of denying tenure to qualified colleagues and creating vacan-
> cies available for hiring economists of their own ilk.

All three positive personnel committee recommendations
were upheld by the dean's-level personnel committee with strong

positive votes. Department Chairman Aitken and Dean Alfange also supported tenure and promotion. However, with the substantial numbers of negative votes at the Department level, Provost Gluckstern questioned tenure and promotion for Tsao and Wright. At this point, 21 out of 22 of the full-time economics faculty members in residence signed a petition urging the University administration to support the Department's decisions granting tenure and promotion in all three cases. Aitken and Alfange added further memoranda in support of Tsao and Wright. Nevertheless, Gluckstern still recommended against tenure for them. However, after conversations with a number of people involved in the Tsao and Wright tenure deliberations at the department and dean levels, the chancellor of the Amherst campus, Randolph W. Bromery reversed Gluckstern's recommendation, and all three faculty members were given tenure by the board of trustees and promoted to associate professor.

A number of plausible elements possibly played into this reversal. First, it is unlikely that the chancellor would have reversed the decisions of the provost without strong support for Tsao and Wright from the Department chairman and the dean of the Faculty of Social and Behavioral Sciences. That support was unequivocal and vigorous. Apart from the fact that the two believed that tenure and promotion for both were well deserved, they may also have been concerned, like some nonradical faculty, that the negative votes on the Department personnel committee might have been politically or ideologically motivated, even though, as previously noted, different standards could have explained the same result. Political or ideological motivation, of course, is exactly what Alfange and the administration thought had interfered with respect to the two Departmental recommendations of denial of reappointment of Best when Kindahl and Rottenberg were Department heads. Now the worry, possibly shared by Bromery, might have been that the same thing could be happening but this time coming from the other side. Many years later, in e-mail correspondence (May 2, 2008), Alfange wrote:

> ...I was particularly concerned that personnel decisions in the Department not be based on political or ideological considerations. I had pledged to the Department that I would make every effort to insure that the fears expressed by Professor Holesovsky would not become reality, and I regarded it as essential that the radicals be prevented from practicing reverse discrimination if they should be inclined to do so. I do not recall whether I saw reverse discrimination as a factor in the Tsao and Wright cases, but surely it could have been perceived that way, and I knew it was vitally important to avoid that perception.[10]

In addition, two radical faculty members on the Department personnel committee (the same two in each tenure case) had second thoughts about the weakly positive votes on Tsao and Wright, coming to believe that they were mistakes and that the two men deserved tenure. These views were communicated to Bromery.

Thus, although the two earlier denials of reappointment of the radical Best by Department nonradicals had been reversed by the administration partly out of fear that the decisions were politically or ideologically motivated, the same fear may have played a role in the chancellor's decision not to uphold Gluckstern's support of the negative votes by Department radicals on the tenure and promotion of nonradicals Tsao and Wright. But regardless of whether politics or ideology figured into the casting of those negative votes, the clash of differing standards for tenure and promotion adhered to by

10. Reproduced in slightly modified form with permission.

the two sides was a major hurdle that the Department was, at that moment, unable to overcome. In spite of the granting, in the end, of tenure and promotion to all three faculty members, the bitterness left by this disagreement was considerable and the tensions in the Department were as great, if not greater, than those of previous years described earlier.

Return for a moment to the development of the unique graduate program in radical political economy with its alternative paradigmatic approaches. In the discussions out of which that program emerged, the issue of the role of neoclassical economics in the graduate program was intensely debated among the radical faculty. The primary point of contention was standard microeconomic analysis. On the grounds of its irrelevance, from the radical perspective, to understanding economic reality, the case was made for its complete elimination. But those in favor of retaining it as an integral part of the PhD program argued that the Department would not really have a graduate program in economics without it. Nor would the economics profession be likely to recognize it as such. Since microeconomics was taught to undergraduates at virtually every university in the country, the Department's PhD students would have difficulty finding academic jobs if they were not certified to teach the subject at least at the very elementary levels. Moreover, because the Department's graduates would probably reject microeconomic theory entirely and spend at least some portion of their careers criticizing it, as part of their training as scholars they, of necessity, had to know something about what they were rejecting and criticizing. It was also important that they be able to compare microeconomic theory to the theories of radical political economy that they were studying. The arguments to retain microeconomics won the day, and all graduate students were required to take courses and pass examinations in that field.

In spite of the agreement to retain microeconomic analysis in the graduate program, there were still substantial problems to be faced in teaching it. First, the graduate students often tended to be hostile to microeconomic theory and, in their hostility, to make life somewhat unpleasant for the instructors teaching it. The students frequently asked questions and challenged the answers on grounds that went well beyond the boundaries of what a normal course in microeconomic theory, even from a leftist perspective, set out to do. They also questioned what was being taught and what was being left out. They did not see why they had to learn material that seemed totally irrelevant to them, and they had to be repeatedly reminded of its importance by the radical faculty. Second, with faculty movement into and out of the Department as a result of the constant tension and turmoil over the years, the instructors teaching microeconomic theory at the graduate level were constantly changing. Because different instructors emphasized different things, and since those instructors wrote the comprehensive examination in microeconomic theory, the changing instructors made it difficult for graduate students to determine what they should learn and to pass the comprehensive examination in that area. Lastly, during this period the instructors teaching the subject were generally at less than full rank and were not known primarily as microeconomic theorists. As a result, they were unable to command the respect of the graduate students. Clearly, an instructor was needed who would remain in the Department for several years and who the radical graduate students would see as having the same stature as the radical faculty. That instructor would have to have an acknowledged commitment to microeconomic theory. He or she would also have to be a full professor in order not to reinforce the impression that microeconomic theory was not especially important to the PhD program. Therefore, early in 1974, the Department began looking for such a person.

Sometime at the start of 1975 I received a phone call from Department Chairman Aitken asking if I might be interested in the position. In those days, I was known mostly as a microeconomic theorist, was a lecturer in economics[11] at the University of California at San Diego, and was looking for a tenured appointment at full rank. The Department in Amherst had heard of my availability from Sonnenschein who still had connections to the Department through faculty members he met while he was at the University of Massachusetts. At the time of Aitken's call, I was expecting an offer with tenure from the Economics Department of the University of Illinois at Chicago. But I preferred to live on the East Coast, and the idea of a small New England town was very appealing. I knew nothing of radical economists and radical political economy. After visiting the Amherst campus and gaining some idea of what radical economics was about, I began to realize that some work I had been doing on methodology might have application in the radical political-economy context, a realization, as will be described in the next chapter, that a few years later actually bore fruit. While on campus, Aitken had told me about the tensions and turmoil in the Department. He painted a rather optimistic picture suggesting that much of the difficulty was now over and I, perhaps through naivete or because I wanted to, bought into it. Evidently, I had become quite interested in the position at the University of Massachusetts. When Aitken called me to indicate that a tenured full-professor offer, having been approved by the Department, was in the works, I told him that I would accept it provided it came before I had to respond to the University of Illinois offer that I had received a few weeks earlier. The official offer Aitken referred to was communicated to

11. This was initially intended to be a visiting (full) professor position. But because I had permanently left my previous full professorship at the University of Waterloo and was not, therefore, visiting *from* anywhere, I was given the title of lecturer.

Donald W. Katzner, May 1989, photograph by Randall Bausor. *(From the collection of the author)*

me over the telephone just in time, and I took up my position in the University of Massachusetts' Economics Department the following September of 1975.

I arrived in Amherst to confront a decidedly complex situation. Department faculty members were outwardly friendly but seemed to be gingerly treading on eggshells in their relationships with one another. There were thinly covered-over tensions lurking just below the surface and raw wounds that no one wanted to reopen. The recent exodus from the Department of nonradical faculty had continued, and those who had stayed or not yet left (Tsao and Wright would also be gone soon) did not want another tumultuously bitter year like 1974–1975. The graduate students, too, were calm and cooperative. Outstanding microeconomic theory problems in the graduate program were resolved in the fall by providing one course and a comprehensive examination for the large number of second-year-and-beyond students who, for one reason or another, had not yet satisfied their microeconomics requirement. The first-year students had their own first-year microeconomics course in the spring. Both courses and the comprehensive went smoothly. I actually enjoyed teaching these courses and, as I indicated in Chapter 1, found the questioning of the students both interesting and stimulating. That year I also served as chair of the Department's personnel and executive committees. But nothing of any consequence ever came up.

However, one significant matter did arise in the Department during 1975–1976. Aitken, who had had his fill of Departmental turmoil and politics over the last three years (one as administrative officer under Alfange, and two as Department chair) and was facing difficult personal problems, submitted his resignation from the chair position effective September 1, 1976. Glen Gordon, another political scientist who was replacing Alfange and serving as acting dean of the Faculty of Social and Behavioral Sciences, appointed a search committee to find a new chair. All major viewpoints in the Department, including those of the radical and nonradical faculty (and their subfactions) and those of the graduate and undergraduate students, were represented. The administration was tired of the fighting within the Department, and the number of full-time faculty members had shrunk to a dangerous low while undergraduate enrollments had soared (as the administration had hoped with the hiring of the radical package). The Department was told that, if it could resolve the internal differences that had created so much difficulty in the past, it would be given as many as ten new positions to fill, with at least one at full rank. In this offer a number of faculty members perceived an implicit threat: If the Department could not put its act together and overcome its internal problems, the prospect of breaking up and disbanding the Department might be considered in which the radicals would be moved to the Political

Science Department and the nonradicals transferred to what was then called the School of Business Administration. The unique radical PhD program in economics would be terminated. This threat, whether real or only imagined, was taken seriously, especially by the radicals. As previously described, they had something in the Economics Department that they considered to be extremely important and exciting and that did not exist anywhere else. They thought that if the Department were to be broken up and disbanded, they would lose practically everything they had gained in moving to the University of Massachusetts.

The search committee's report was completed and approved by the Department and Dean Gordon in the spring of 1976. However, with the considerable and long-standing tensions in the Department, the committee recognized that it had to do much more than just that for which it was charged. Accordingly, the introduction to its report states:

> ...because of unique problems within the Department whose basis
> extends well over five years in the past, the Committee realized that
> it had to do more than simply choose a chair—it had to create an
> atmosphere of trust and respect among faculty and students and it
> had to unify the Department around the new chair.

Thus, in addition to selecting a new chair, the committee placed specific faculty members in administrative positions and on committees within the Departmental committee structure and set out rules and plans that would make it unnecessary for the radical and nonradical factions to fight over the new hires. As things turned out, the committee's work was largely responsible for making it possible for the Department to overcome its historical turmoil and tensions during the following few years.

The most important recommendation of the search committee was that, out of the ten new hires, three were to be from the area of radical political economics and seven were to be more traditional economists. This meant that, after all new positions were filled and all expected departures (including retirements) occurred, the Department faculty would be composed of 40 percent radical and 60 percent nonradical economists. Although there was no official characterization of the qualities that defined a radical economist as distinct from a nonradical economist, the particular classification of each faculty member present at the time as radical or nonradical was understood and accepted by everyone in the Department. The search committee report also stated that, were faculty departures to occur in the future, radicals would be replaced by radicals and non-radicals by nonradicals. Equally important as the 40 percent–60 percent division, it was implicit in this arrangement that all new hires for radical positions as well as tenure and promotion decisions relating to radicals would be controlled by the radical faculty with full support from the nonradical faculty, and that the nonradical faculty would have similar control and radical-faculty support with respect to nonradical positions and personnel decisions relating to nonradical faculty. These provisions effectively eliminated the clash between differing standards for personnel actions that had plagued the Department when Best, Tsao, and Wright were considered for tenure and promotion almost two years earlier. Generally, the search committee's assignments to departmental administrative positions and committees achieved an appropriate balance of radical and non-radical faculty. In particular, the personnel committee, which was to be combined with the executive committee and would deal with all important Departmental matters including hiring, was to contain faculty representatives of all major departmental perspectives. No graduate students were placed on any committee.[12] However, the search committee expressed the hope that communications between faculty and students would be sufficient so that student objectives and concerns could be heard and explored. (Nevertheless, graduate students would be invited to attend, on a regular basis, certain committee meetings in later years.) Perhaps because I was new and, therefore, contrary to other economics faculty, had none of the historical baggage relating to past battles in the Department, and perhaps because my newness permitted me to speak comfortably with everyone, I was asked to be Department chair.

It was a flattering offer that, for obvious reasons, I had no choice but to accept. However, the job was not going to be easy. Somehow, in spite of the simmering resentment still harbored by many faculty, the Department had to demonstrate that it could run its affairs in a unified way without coming near to or crossing into the territory of self-destruction. The blueprint had been created by the search committee. It was now time to make it work.

12. During these early years, the graduate students debated among themselves whether they should push for representation on faculty committees, and they decided against it. At that time, they desired to maintain their independence, and did not want the Department to be able to say that a particular committee decision was favored by the graduate students because a token student representative was present when the decision was made. Later on, however, their reluctance to serve on faculty committees changed considerably.

Chapter 8

Learning to Live Together

I officially took up my duties as chair on September 1, 1976, feeling somewhat uncomfortable and inadequate.[1] Apart from my previous year as chair of the Department's personnel and executive committees (both of which did very little), I had not yet in my academic career served on a single Departmental administrative committee or in any Departmental administrative position or capacity. Now, suddenly, I was responsible for the operation of an entire Department. Fortunately, I had inherited an excellent secretary, Annia Balon, who knew what paperwork had to be done. However, the job turned out to be much more than moving paper, which I learned how to do very quickly. It was mostly politics—working out conflicts and problems as they arose, and trying to anticipate possible future conflicts and problems and prevent them from happening. And then, in addition, there were the ten positions to be filled (more if any current faculty members resigned).

In the resolution of conflicts and problems, I had the full support of the administration. Acting dean Gordon had been replaced as dean of the Faculty of Social and Behavioral Sciences by another acting dean, also as of September 1, 1976. The new acting dean was Thomas O. Wilkinson, a sociologist. He became permanent dean on September 1, 1979. Over the years, Wilkinson gave me the flexibility and backing that were needed to reach compromises between

---

1. I had actually begun to do the work of the chair two months earlier.

the radicals and nonradicals when significant divisions arose. When necessary, he advocated for those compromises at higher administrative levels. Wilkinson also was a big help in defending the Department from several seemingly right-wing political attacks that came from different quarters within the University.

I served as Department chair for five years through the summer of 1981. From beginning to end I had the sense that the economics faculty was trying very hard to get along with each other and overcome its history of turmoil and tensions. The turmoil and tensions that did arise during the period stemmed from vastly different perceptions of what was important and of the way the world and, in particular, the Department operated or should have operated. These perceptions were deeply felt on both sides—radical and nonradical. They were honest differences, honestly represented, that had to be dealt with. Of course, there were major battles—actually, one each year for the first three years—as I will describe below. However, through them all, in spite of the intensity of feelings and discussions (and that intensity was, at times, considerable), there was mutual respect and sensitivity, serious efforts to understand the opposing side's position, and a willingness to compromise. There were times when I thought that the Department was going to come apart, but it never happened. In the end, everyone pulled together and began to appreciate and, to some extent, even enjoy one another's work and company. Intellectual discussions across boundaries became commonplace and productive, and the academic environment truly exciting as the near perfection earlier achieved among the radical faculty spread to include nonradicals. Radicals and nonradicals really did learn to live together.

The radical-nonradical interaction noted here took on a variety of forms. That in the classroom, indirectly between nonradical and radical faculty through graduate student intermediaries and directly between nonradical faculty and radical graduate students has been described in Chapter 1. As a further illustration, Douglas Vickers,[2] a nonradical full professor, had many conversations with Steven A. Resnick and Richard D. Wolff (who were associated with the Marxism-mutual-interaction paradigm) on the one hand, and with James R. Crotty (who was identified with the Marxism-Keynesian-macroeconomics paradigm) on the other. From his nonradical perspective, Vickers was thinking about the impact of historical time, ignorance, and nonprobabilistic uncertainty on human decision making.[3] Resnick and Wolff were dealing with similar concepts in their mutually interactive approach, and Crotty was examining them in the Marxism-Keynesian macroeconomic context. Each had read a significant portion of the other's work, and in both cases, each had found considerable interest and appreciation in what the other was doing.

I also had considerable direct interaction with the radical faculty. Before arriving on campus, I had been investigating methodologies for analyzing, without trying to measure, phenomenon for which measures of the relevant variables were not available.[4] During my first year in the University of Massachusetts Economics Department, I discovered that Herbert Gintis was trying to understand certain social interactions within the economic firm that were clearly not quantifiable in any known way. We worked together on this problem, eventually publishing a jointly authored paper, "Profits, Optimality, and the Social Division of Labour in the Firm"

---

2. Vickers joined the Economics Department in January of 1978. He received his PhD degree from the University of London and, before coming to Amherst, had been Professor of Finance at the University of Pennsylvania and Professor of Economics at the University of Western Australia.

3. For a brief statement of what these concepts involve, see note 6 in the next chapter.

4. Later published as *Analysis without Measurement* (Cambridge: Cambridge University Press, 1983).

in *Sociological Economics*, L. Lévy-Garboua, ed. (London: Sage, 1979), pp. 269–297. This effort opened up a new line of research for me that I pursued along a variety of paths for several years. Frequent conversations with Resnick and Wolff resulted in my providing them with extensive comments on one of their books, and my including a summary of their Marxism-mutual-interaction perspective in a published discussion of alternative approaches to economic analysis.[5]

Lastly, numerous conversations with Samuel S. Bowles over many years have had a significant impact on us both. Two results of those conversations that actually came to fruition some years after the period of time under consideration here were as follows: On the one hand, Bowles read and commented on several papers I had written concerning organization problems within the economic firm. At one point he made me aware of the Condorcet Jury Theorem (the proposition that the probability that a group of voting individuals choosing between two options will collectively make the "correct" decision[6] rises with the size of the majority). That hint led me to consider the application of that theorem to describing properties of the most appropriate locations or levels in a firm's hierarchical authority structure for the making of decisions. It turned out that the optimal location for making a specific decision may actually be different from the location at which the probability of making the correct decision is the highest. In particular, since employees lower down often have less costly access to information and are paid less than higher management, the optimal location may be biased away

5. "Alternatives to Equilibrium Analysis," *Eastern Economic Journal*, 11 (1985): 404–421. Reprinted in Chapter 1 of my *Time, Ignorance, and Uncertainty in Economic Models* (Ann Arbor: University of Michigan Press, 1998).
6. It is assumed that sometime in the future when the consequences of the actual decision made are known, it will be possible to determine which of the two choices was the right or correct decision to make and which was not.

from the level of highest probability of correctness in a downward direction toward the shop floor.[7] On the other hand, Bowles has given me credit for playing a role in his coming to understand the generic significance of the general equilibrium theory of the neoclassical paradigm,[8] a topic which he addressed in his *Microeconomics: Behavior, Institutions, and Evolution* (New York: Russell Sage, Princeton: Princeton University Press, 2004). In an electronic mail message to a student that he shared with me, Bowles wrote: "The only thing that economists know that other social scientists and historians do not is general equilibrium. It's too important to be left to the... general equilibrium theorists."[9]

The three major battles alluded to earlier, and to be referred to in what follows, all occurred between the radical graduate students and the economics faculty. (Recall that, by now, the graduate student body was largely radical.) Each battle placed the radical wing of the faculty in a very uncomfortable position. That was because, in every case, the radical faculty was highly sympathetic with at least some aspects of the goals that the radical students were pursuing. Because the radical graduate students were more closely allied with the radical rather than the nonradical faculty, and because the radical faculty obviously had more power over the radical graduate

---

7. This will be the case when the criterion for determining the location is that of maximizing the expected value of the decision net of the costs involved in making and implementing it. In that circumstance, the rising cost of making and implementing the decision as the hierarchical level increases toward upper management has to be balanced against the rising and then falling expected value of the decision (before deduction of the costs of making and implementing it) as the hierarchical level rises and crosses the level at which the probability of correctness is the highest. Here the phrase *expected value of the decision* refers to the sum of (1) the value outcome of the decision project less its operating costs when the decision is, in fact, correct, multiplied by the probability of correctness, and (2) the value outcome of the decision project less its operating costs when the decision is incorrect, multiplied by the probability that the decision made is incorrect. See my "Participation and the Location of Decision-Making in the Firm," *Journal of Comparative Economics* 27 (1999): 150–167.

8. Electronic mail communication to a student dated October 16, 2007.

9. Ibid. Reproduced with permission.

students than did the nonradical faculty, these three battles were resolved by bringing enough pressure to bear on the radical faculty so that the latter would persuade the radical graduate students to compromise or give in. Of course, putting pressure on the radical faculty was a delicate matter, usually requiring considerable thought and careful action. Likewise, the radical faculty had to tread gingerly when pushing the radical graduate students to cooperate in ending the battle. The first battle was, by far, the most severe. Each subsequent battle had a little less intensity than the preceding one.

The pressures brought to bear on the radical faculty to resolve the issues over which the battles were fought rested implicitly on the threats, partly described at the end of Chapter 7, of the dissolution of the Department and the loss of the unique radical PhD program in alternative paradigmatic approaches. These threats were perceived as stemming from both internal and external sources. The internal threat arose, as previously described, from the possibility that the Department would be unable to resolve its own internal difficulties, thus giving the administration the incentive to split it into two parts and terminate the radical PhD program in economics. The external threat was that if the Department were too loud and too publicly radical in its ways, the outside world might, in the then-current environment of fear of the Soviet Union and Communism, perceive it as dangerous. In that event, politicians would then have an incentive to pressure the University to break up the Department and get rid of the radical political economists. As previously suggested, these threats were important motivating forces in the willingness of the radical wing of the faculty to compromise because the radical faculty had something of great significance and importance to them that they did not want to lose.

Before explicitly describing the aforementioned battles and other Department events, two additional points are worth making.

First, in spite of its general radical perspective, the graduate student body was seriously split in a variety of ways. These splits arose, not only from political and ideological differences that are typically present within many groups of individuals, but also from shifting personal relations and alliances between individual graduate students and various radical faculty members that sometimes generated jealousies and anger. As a result, it was often difficult for the graduate students to present a united front on questions that impinged on things that the graduate students felt were important to them and on graduate-student-to-faculty and graduate-student-to-Department relations. The presence of such splits, of course, often made it considerably easier for the economics faculty to overcome graduate student opposition on contentious matters. There were, of course, a few exceptions in which the graduate students were solidly together. These occurred largely when there was a clear student-against-faculty issue and, with respect to that issue, the students felt under attack by the faculty. For example, as previously indicated, the allocations of teaching assistants to courses (subject to faculty veto) had been delegated to EGSO in the 1974–1975 academic year. The graduate students were unified and fought hard to retain what they considered to be their right to assign teaching assistants to courses whenever they thought that the faculty was going to water down or take that right away.

Second, it is clear that the radical faculty had much in common ideologically and politically with the radical graduate students. However, the two groups had different interests that stemmed mostly from the fact that the faculty were committed to the Economics Department for a much longer period of time (if not their entire careers) than the graduate students who were a part of the Department for only the few years necessary to fulfill the requirements for their degrees. This, in light of the threats noted earlier, meant that the radical faculty were prepared to join with the nonradical faculty on a number of issues, such as what constitutes a dissertation and the proprieties of teaching-assistant-to-faculty relations in courses to which the teaching assistants were assigned. The graduate students did not fully realize the impact of these contrasting interests, and so it was often difficult for them to understand why the radical faculty, who were frequently similar to them in ideology and political approach, at various times opposed them on important Departmental questions. As a result, some graduate students concluded that it was inflexibility and unwillingness on the part of the entire economics faculty (not only the radicals) to explore issues important to them, and the adherence by that faculty to traditional academic norms, which made necessary the graduate student actions that precipitated the battles. Some graduate students felt so strongly in opposition on one or more of the specific issues involved that they left the Department without completing the requirements for a degree.

The first major battle occurred almost immediately after I officially became chair. The Department's head clerk, the senior member of the Department's secretarial staff, had resigned to accept another job elsewhere and needed to be replaced. I began a search in which anyone, inside or outside the Department could apply. Acting on their belief that they should play a significant role in the administration of the Department (recall Chapters 1 and 7), the radical graduate students, through EGSO, selected a candidate within the Department's remaining secretarial staff to support. Their logic, emerging from general radical sympathies with the conventions and practices of labor unions, was that, because their candidate had seniority, having been on the Department's staff the longest, she should be appointed to the head clerk position. However, in my judgment (and that of most other faculty members as well) the person involved did not have the qualifications or the skills to do the job. That individual, herself, also had considerable doubts about whether she was up to it. But the graduate students convinced her that she could handle the assignment, and they persuaded the other members of the secretarial staff to support her, too. With the graduate students and secretarial staff pushing hard for their candidate to be appointed, there was considerable pressure on me and the faculty to accede to their wishes.

I flatly refused and began to interview outside applicants. It did not take long to find a highly qualified and skilled candidate. However, I could not act without the support of the full faculty in resolving the problem with the radical graduate students, and the radical wing of the faculty was reluctant to oppose the radical graduate students with whom they were moderately sympathetic. Something needed to be done that would induce the radical faculty to put pressure on the radical graduate students to back off. Weeks passed. With the intense lobbying by the radical graduate students and the secretarial staff that was going on, little administrative work was being done. Among many other things, there were the ten positions given to us by the dean that we needed to begin the process of filling, but we could not devote serious attention to them because of the time and energy that the head-clerk problem required.

One of the individuals on the radical side of the Department with whom I had become quite friendly during the previous year was Resnick. Resnick understood the problem and was trying to come up with a way that would give the radical faculty the leverage they needed to convince the radical graduate students to stop their efforts to secure the head clerk position for their candidate. One night in the middle of October, Resnick, who during this period lived in Boston but often remained in Amherst for several days at a time, was sleeping at my house. That evening we spent several hours talking about what to do without coming up with any ideas. Upon waking in the morning, both of us had independently and simultaneously arrived at the same solution: I would tell the Department that I would resign from the chair position if the radical faculty would not support me and the radical graduate students would not back off. Of course, threats of resignation are credible only if they are backed by significant consequences and used very rarely. This threat was both credible and serious, not only because I had been chair for only a few weeks, but also because it raised in the minds of the radicals the possibility, noted earlier, of the dissolution of the Department and the loss of the radical graduate program. Within two days, the desired result had been achieved, and I hired the outside candidate I had found for the head-clerk position. As part of the (informal) agreement that ended the battle, I asked Dean Wilkinson to find a way to increase the salary of EGSO's candidate. Wilkinson succeeded in doing that by mid January.

The remainder of the 1976–1977 academic year went relatively smoothly. Six positions were filled, two radical and four nonradical. All hires were at the assistant professor or pretenure-track instructor level except one of the nonradical positions, which was filled at full rank with the appointment of Vickers. One of the radical positions was shared by two people—alternately one on leave (but remaining in residence) while the other executing the duties of the position. The radical graduate students had requested to be a part of the hiring process, and that request had been granted. The graduate students participated in the initial interviews of candidates at the annual national convention of economists and were given time to meet and further interview those candidates invited to visit the Department.

In general, relations between radical graduate students assigned as teaching assistants to a course taught by a nonradical faculty member were quite cordial. The former were content to present non-radical material, in their discussion sections, in a reasonably positive manner and grade exams appropriately even though they thought that that nonradical material, if not outright "wrong" as explanation of economic phenomena, was still irrelevant to the economic world as they saw it. However, in the fall of 1977, at least one zealous student overstepped the boundaries of propriety in this regard and set off the second major battle between the faculty and radical graduate students. The graduate student in question denigrated the material taught by the faculty member in the course to which the former was assigned and later on, after grading a midterm exam, refused to show the faculty member the grades he would assign to the students who took the exam.

Not surprisingly, the faculty member was outraged and deeply resentful, and wanted the Department to discipline the student. The radical faculty and many of the radical graduate students also thought this behavior to be improper. However, in keeping with their desire to be involved in Departmental administration, the graduate students wanted a resolution to emerge from negotiations between the two in which another faculty member and another graduate student, neither of whom were involved in any way with the course, participated. The offended faculty member thought that highly inappropriate and refused. It was left to the Department's personnel-executive committee, on which this faculty member happened to serve, to work out a solution. The radical faculty members on that committee were in a delicate position: With the threat from internal disorder lurking in the background, they felt that they had to support the nonradical faculty member, but at the same time, they were sympathetic to and did not want to alienate the radical graduate student body. During the long and intense discussions that ensued, the radical faculty members showed remarkable sensitivity to the passionately held position of the offended nonradical faculty member and successfully prevented their own serious estrangement from the radical graduate students. A memorandum from me dated September 29, 1977 that had the unanimous support of the personnel-executive committee set out the proper role of graduate students assigned as teaching assistants in courses and, by clear implication, condemned the above behavior. In the end the offending graduate student ceased denigrating the course material and turned over his grades to the faculty member teaching the course.

The resolution of this conflict between the nonradical faculty member and radical graduate student seemed to have emotionally exhausted the faculty on the personnel-executive committee which, recall, was also in charge of recruiting new faculty. That exhaustion left the nonradical faculty on the committee unable to agree on any appointment to fill a nonradical position. There was one outstanding candidate who might have been interested in coming to the University of Massachusetts, but one nonradical faculty member thought that he might be radical. No one had enough emotional energy to investigate the extent to which this might actually have been true and, were it not true, to persuade the nonradical faculty member to change his mind. However, the Department did hire an assistant professor to fill the last open radical position.

Two other events that occurred during 1977–1978 are worthy of note. First, the School of Business Administration required (and still does) their undergraduate students to take the Economics Department's introductory microeconomics and introductory macroeconomics courses as part of their degree. However, in February of 1978, the acting dean of that School sent a memorandum to its faculty asking them to identify instances of "Marxist emphasis" in those courses. The Department's introductory courses were (and still are) intended to provide students with the basic substance and techniques of standard economic analysis on which the material of more advanced business and economics courses could be built. The Department was putting its best teachers in those courses, some of whom were radical and all of whom were scrupulously living up to the courses' standards and aims. The implied attack from the School of Business Administration may have been politically motivated but, in any case, it was very quickly deflected (before the Department could mount its own response) by a memorandum dated March 3, 1978 from Acting Dean Wilkinson in which he pointed out that the offending memorandum raised very serious issues of academic freedom.

The second noteworthy event of that year was that the Department received enormous national and world-wide publicity in a highly favorable article that appeared in *Science Magazine,* 199 (January 6, 1978): 34–38, under the title, "Radicals at Universities: 'Critical Mass' at U. Mass." That article, written within the broader context of radicals at universities in general, not only described the character of and some of the intellectual excitement in the University of Massachusetts' Amherst Economics Department, but it also briefly summarized the history of the hiring of the radical package.

By the end of the spring semester of 1978, radical and nonradical faculty members had become sufficiently comfortable with each other to be able, in the following fall, to invite a representative of EGSO to attend many of the Department's personnel-executive committee discussions.

Perhaps stemming, in part, from their interest in poverty and inequality, expanding academic opportunities for women and minorities, or the pursuit of what have been referred to as "affirmative action" programs, was a high priority among both the radical faculty and radical graduate students. For the Economics Department, this had meant careful attention to expanding the pool of candidates to include as many women and minorities as possible in hiring faculty and admitting graduate students. The radical graduate students were especially zealous in this regard, often adding many names for the Department to consider. However, in the fall of 1978, in trying to expand the pool of applicants to the PhD program in economics, some of the radical graduate students wanted EGSO, at its expense, to place an ad in the *Boston Globe,* one of Boston's major newspapers, seeking applications,. This touched a raw nerve in the economics faculty and ignited the third major battle between faculty and graduate students cited earlier.

It was not that the economics faculty did not want to advertise and draw in as many applicants as possible. But in the then-current environment of fear of the Soviet Union and Communism, it did not seem prudent to flaunt the existence, at the University of Massachusetts (a public institution), of a radical PhD program in economics with its intellectual ties to Marxism, directly under the noses of state politicians and the Massachusetts public. The radical faculty were wary of the potential damage that this could do to their presence at the University and the radical PhD program, and they did not need any pressure from the nonradical faculty to try to stop it. However, they had to be careful because they sympathized with the general means and the ends of affirmative action programs and, as before, they did not want to incense or estrange the radical graduate students. Nevertheless, once again, they were successful in dealing with the radical graduate students, and the ad never appeared in the *Boston Globe.*

Also in the fall of 1978, the Department's graduate program was reviewed and evaluated by an outside visitation committee that consisted of Kenneth J. Arrow (Harvard), Donald J. Harris (Stanford), and Michael J. Piore (M.I.T). This was the first review and evaluation since that of the fall of 1970 that preceded Kindahl's resignation as Department head. It was also the first review and evaluation of the Department since the departure of its earlier contingent of well-known and highly regarded nonradical economists and its reconstitution with a "critical mass" of radical political economists. The report of the visitation committee, received on November 20, 1978, was generally quite positive. Among other things it stated that (p. 1):

> The Department of Economics appears to be vigorous and healthy. It is comprised of a faculty of creative and original scholars, whose international reputation lies in economic research as well as [in] a strong commitment to teaching at both the graduate and undergraduate levels. The graduate student body compares favorably, in terms of their formal credentials, with any graduate student body in the country.... [There is] a deep and personal commitment... [among faculty and graduate students] to the development of an understanding of the economy and society, to their own scholarly work and to the Department as an institution. The students are highly motivated, bright, articulate, opinionated and argumentative, but are remarkably open to a wide range of different ideas.

The report also describes a number of negatives, such as the necessary sacrifice (due to lack of resources and graduate student time) of extensive training in microeconomic theory and of certain applied fields in order to provide courses in political economy. Several other negatives that the report identifies are obvious from previous discussion here and in earlier chapters, but, in general, the report concludes that (p. 4):

> ...the explicit commitment of a large part of the faculty and virtually all the student body to radical or Marxist economics does not appear to have outweighed the curriculum in that direction

and that (p. 13)

> ...the development of the graduate program in economics in the
> last five years is something in which the University of Massachusetts
> can take considerable pride.

However, the following May 15, the acting dean of the Graduate
School filed his position paper that concluded the review process. Whether intentional or not, it could only be described as an
unconscionable affront to, and political attack on the Department.
Quoting from my description of the position paper in a memo to
the economics faculty dated May, 21, 1979, that paper

> ...is replete with internal contradictions and inaccurate facts.... [It]
> asserts without documentation that the quality of our graduate stu-
> dents is not high enough, that the graduate students rather than the
> faculty run the Department, that we are proselytizing rather than
> teaching in the classroom, that we are not doing enough research,
> and so on. There are also the suggestions that the kind of research
> we do undertake is inappropriate, and that we are unable to place
> our graduate students [in appropriate jobs].

Dean Wikinson played a key role in having this report with-
drawn and rewritten. The rewritten position paper (June 5, 1979)
did not contain the offensive and inaccurate language of the original, although, in the opinion of the economics faculty, it still emphasized too much of the negative in a very positive visitation-commit-
tee report.

The 1978–1979 academic year also saw continued increases
in the Department's undergraduate enrollments. Two nonradical
assistant professors were hired. But over the previous three years

there were also departures of nonradical faculty. Some of these were due to the availability of what were seen as better opportunities. Others were a consequence of earlier Department fights that had left the departed faculty members looking for new positions. The result was that more than the original seven nonradical hires promised by Acting Dean Gordon were needed to bring the nonradical side of the Department up to full strength.

The last two years of my tenure as Department chair were not nearly as difficult as the first three. There was one minor political attack during the period. Upon reading an article in *Business Week* (April 28, 1980) that briefly mentioned that Bowles was a Marxist and in the Economics Department on the Amherst campus of the University of Massachusetts, a "concerned citizen" wrote to the University's provost, Loren Baritz, inquiring about whether "our campuses are invaded by Communists."[10] Baritz responded in a letter dated December 31, 1980 by defending Bowles's work and radical political economy as a legitimate part of economics that is recognized as important nationally. He also defended the principle of academic freedom and the importance of having alternative viewpoints represented in university environments.

There were, in addition, minor problems with the radical graduate students. In one instance Vaclav Holesovsky, the nonradical economist, was teaching a course in Marxian economics and, rather suddenly, became seriously ill and died in the middle of the spring semester. Now, the nonradical approach to Marxian economics was considerably different from the radical approach. Although the students in the course had already spent half of the semester studying the nonradical approach, only graduate students who subscribed to the radical approach were available for replacing the instructor. Moreover,

10. Letter from Mrs. H.L. Robb dated November 18, 1980.

time was of the essence. With the consent of the faculty, I acted quickly to install a highly competent, advanced graduate student, David F. Ruccio, who was quite sympathetic and sensitive to the problem that the students in the course would face. However, EGSO wanted to have a say in the replacement process and protested my action. (There was no complaint about the specific choice of a replacement.) They were also concerned that my proceeding without student input in placing a graduate student as an instructor in a course might limit their role in assigning teaching assistants to courses and faculty. However, after acknowledging their protest and indicating that my action was directed only toward the timely resolution of an emergency, the issue was quickly dropped. In a second instance, several overzealous graduate students, meaning no harm, staged an unannounced "guerilla" invasion of a classroom as a demonstration of revolutionary activity. Many students in the course were upset and frightened. After making sure that the students involved, including the teaching assistant in charge, understood how inappropriate and serious this was, a letter of apology was sent to all of the students over the signatures of the teaching assistant in charge, myself, and Dean Wilkinson.

Finally, two nonradical assistant professors were hired during 1979–1980 and one more the following academic year. And the radicals decided that the two individual radical political economists, hired during 1976–1977, who were sharing one radical position, should each be given a full radical position as soon as such a position became available either from a resignation or from departmental growth.[11]

I left the chair position on September 1, 1981, emotionally drained. During the previous five years, the Department had

---

11. The size of the radical wing of the Department was to remain at 40 percent of the total economics faculty.

calmed considerably. Trust between the radical and nonradical wings had grown. Both undergraduate enrollments and the size of the faculty had expanded substantially. There were still problems to be faced, but there was the feeling shared by most faculty that the Department had passed a difficult test and had prospered while doing so. The intellectual excitement generated by the great diversity in the Department and the near perfection achieved was a source of pleasure and optimism shared by many.

Chapter 9

Epilogue

Don't let it be forgot
That once there was a spot
For one brief shining moment that was known
As Camelot.

A.J. Lerner and F. Lowe, Camelot

In our world, perfection, no matter how closely approximated, cannot last. Outside events, changing circumstances, and human development, frailties, and weaknesses always intervene to cause its disruption and dissipation. That happened to Arthur's Camelot, and it happened to the Economics Department on the University of Massachusetts' Amherst campus.

Up to the mid 1980s, the Department had been run mostly by those older individuals who had joined the economics faculty by 1975 and who had played a major role in working out compromises between radicals and nonradicals from 1975 to 1980. By 1985, however, the younger generation in the Department, many of whom had been hired more recently and had been given, or were close to being given, tenure by then, were becoming restless. As of 1980 they were not quite yet mature scholars, and many had come late to the exciting and stimulating intellectual intercourse that had developed among radicals and between some radicals and some nonradicals during the 1970s. Thus, even if these younger faculty members were teaching graduate courses, they had still been largely left out of much of the latter discussions and interactions. Not surprisingly, the younger generation wanted to be more a part of the Department and to have more of a say in running it. They also began to dislike being identified as radical or nonradical according to the classification scheme set up in the search-committee report of the spring of 1976. The aversion to that scheme arose because the younger faculty members felt that they were more flexible and eclectic than the rigid and narrow classification scheme made them out to be. The impetus for these latter feelings may have had something to do with what was then occurring in the outside world. First, this generation was too young for the Civil Rights and Vietnam War protest movements, now in the distant past, to have had a major impact on their lives. Second, the threat of Communism and the fear of the Soviet Union had begun to decline, weakening the allure of Marxism and interest in traditional radical topics like imperialism. Moreover, some Marxian ideas, such as power and authority in the firm, intergenerational inequality, and unemployment as labor discipline, had been picked up by economists with little or no intellectual connection to Marx.[1] Third, with the U.S. economy starting to recover from its inflationary and recessionary difficulties of the previous ten years, domestic economic issues that had initially piqued the curiosity of the radicals, such as poverty, had

1. With respect to power and authority see, for example, M.J. Beckmann, *Rank in Organizations* (Berlin: Springer, 1978) and O.E. Williamson, *Markets and Hierarchies: Analysis and Antitrust Implications* (New York: Free Press, 1975). The embracing of intergenerational inequality can be seen in, say, G.S. Becker and N. Tomes, "Human Capital and the Rise and Fall of Families," *Journal of Labor Economics* 4 (1986): s1–s39. An illustration of the appearance of the labor discipline idea within establishment work may be found in C. Shapiro and J.E. Stiglitz, "Equilibrium Unemployment as a Worker Discipline Device," *American Economic Review* 74 (1984): 433–444.

became less urgent. Of course, the fall of the Berlin wall in 1989, the subsequent breaking away of Eastern Europe from the Soviet umbrella, the collapse of the Soviet Union itself in 1991, and the continuing economic expansion into the 1990s only intensified these feelings.

What was becoming clear was that this subgroup of the economics faculty (along with some of the older faculty members as will be described below) had begun to perceive the field of radical political economics in a new and different way. From their developing perspective, the field was moving closer to the economics establishment (as the establishment, noted earlier, was co-opting some radical notions) both in taking up, albeit in a different way, some of the topics investigated by that establishment, and in adopting some of the establishment's analytical techniques, like the theory of games, as the basis for addressing their own questions. These changes, set in motion in the 1980s, extended well beyond the Economics faculty at the University of Massachusetts at Amherst. They evolved over the next twenty years into a full-blown metamorphosis that considerably modified and broadened the field. In its altered and expanded (and contemporary) form it could now be said that

...radical economics comprises a broad set of methodological approaches, including Marxian political economy, institutionalism, post-Keynesianism, analytical political economy, radical feminism, and post-modernism.... [It] emphasizes conflict outside of class conflict [such as that arising from race and gender relations], policy-relevant analysis, and incorporation of more mainstream methods into radical research.... [Its] characterization of the core injustice of capitalism has moved from a narrowly defined concept of exploitation at the point of production to broader inequality beyond both production and class.... The role of individual choice... has become more prominent... [and the representation of capitalism itself more realistic].[2]

Perhaps because of its expanded intellectual domain, radical political economics has come to be known as heterodox economics.[3]

At any rate, by 1989, restlessness among the younger faculty had built up to the point at which they had become receptive to Departmental change. And while this receptiveness was developing, the intellectual stances of some of the older radical faculty were also evolving in a similar way, thereby providing leadership for a demand for change. As previously noted, Rapping abandoned the field of radical political economics entirely and moved back into closer alignment with the economics establishment. And Bowles and Gintis lost interest in traditional Marxian political economics and began to turn their attention to such topics as altruism in economic behavior and contract enforcement in the labor market. In addressing these and other matters, they employed game theory as one of their fundamental analytical tools. Such intellectual transformations, occurring as they were among both young and older faculty, caused within the Economics Department some of the previously existing sharp paradigmatic distinctions described in Chapter 1 to blur. The exciting and stimulating intra-Departmental discourse that went with those distinctions, and that characterize the near perfection that the Economics Department had achieved, began to dissipate. There was still, to be sure, lively scholarly interaction in the Department, but it did not have the same passion, intensity, and urgency as before.

2. D. Flaherty, Radical Economics, *The New Palgrave Dictionary of Economics*, v. 6, 2nd ed., S.N. Durlauf and L.E. Blume eds. (Houndmills: Palgrave Macmillan, 2008), pp. 835–837.
3. A more detailed and more complete history of heterodox economics, covering, in part, extensive versions of the approaches listed in the previous quotation can be found in F. Lee, *A History of Heterodox Economics* (London: Routledge, 2008).

These intellectual transformations also had an impact on the Department's graduate PhD program and on its radical/nonradical classification scheme. In the spring of 1991 changes were adopted in the former that de-emphasized cross-paradigmatic comparisons and propelled it, in some small measure, toward more traditional programs. Courses taught by Bowles and Gintis began to employ, in confluence with their altered research interests, the methodology of game theory rather than Marxian methodologies. Comprehensive examinations were revised so that students need be examined on economic theory in relation to only one paradigm instead of two. The second examination could now cover an applied field such as economic development, economic history, or labor economics.

A few years later in the spring of 1994, in the process of selecting a new chair, the rule that 40 percent of the Department's faculty should be from the field of radical political economy was discarded:

> Having regard to the evolution of Department members' professional interests, activities, and curriculum developments,... at this time the existing dichotomization of the Department memberships [sic] into [radical] "political economy" [sic] and [non-radical economics is to] be... discontinued. [However] the dedication of the Department to the intellectual diversity and varying professional commitments that have identified the uniqueness of the Department [is to be maintained] ....[4]

The elimination of the 40 percent rule was initiated by the nonradical Douglas Vickers as chairman of the Department's Chair Search Committee and was a reflection of the new harmonies and new

4. Report of the Chair Search Committee, April 8, 1994, p. 5.

interaffiliation of ideas and interests that had come to characterize the Department. Its importance should not be underestimated.
Dropping the 40 percent rule represented closure or the end of the
no-longer-necessary agreements associated with the search-committee report of the spring of 1976 that had permitted the Department
to overcome difficult ideological differences and function as a unified, friendly, and productive unit. It also signaled the end of the
radical era in the Economics Department on the Amherst campus
of the University of Massachusetts as it existed from the early 1970s
into the mid 1980s.

It should also be noted that, by this time, Richard C. Edwards
of the original radical package had left the Department along with
Michael H. Best and two others who had earlier been counted as radical political economists. Leonard A. Rapping had died in October
of 1991. Subsequent retirements have left only Steven A. Resnick
from the radical package as a full-time faculty member. James R.
Crotty retired in 2008. As for those members of the Economics faculty who served as chairmen of the Economics Department, James
K. Kindahl retired from the Department in 1998 and died in 2003.
Simon Rottenberg retired the same year as did Kindahl and lived
until 2004. Norman D. Aitken moved into University administration in 1992 and did not return to the Department as a full-time faculty member. And I am still a full-time member of the Economics
faculty.

However, in spite of all of these changes and departures, the
intellectual legacy left by members of the original radical package,
with the addition of Rapping and Crotty, up through 1981 remains
significant. That legacy includes a sweeping revision and extension of Marxian theory as well as a resuscitation of its notion of the
reserve army of the unemployed, and substantial contributions to
post-Keynesian economic thought, and to the analyses of inflation,

segmented labor markets, endogenous preferences, the economics of education, and the exercise of power in markets with incomplete contracts. Extending their influence still further, the radical faculty created two institutions in the late 1970s that continue to thrive to this day: The Center for Popular Economics reaches into the non-academic community to promote economic justice through education. The Association for Economic and Social Analysis advances the development of the revised version of Marxian theory identified with the Resnick-Wolff paradigm of mutual interaction of all analytical elements, in part with the publication of its widely read journal *Rethinking Marxism*.

There is more. The presence of the radical political economists was the primary contributor to the development of an intellectual ethos or culture that remains in the Economics Department today and that permits serious economic work which, although it does not fall clearly within any of the four main paradigms, is cognate to them. Over the years, multifarious efforts in a variety of fields have been undertaken. Apart from the development of the three radical paradigms listed in Table 1.1 (see p. 15), radical studies in the areas of gender economics, now a part of feminist economics,[5] Latin American development, and the interplay between politics and economics in American capitalism, and extra-paradigmatic collaboration between radicals and nonradicals have already been noted. However, in addition to these latter investigations, inquiries were also undertaken by faculty members who might more readily be classified as closer to the mainstream of economic theory and

5. Feminist economics, as it exists today, challenges neoclassical economic theory in its forceful criticism of that theory's male-focused assumptions. In addition to its gender-economics emphasis on the role of gender as it relates to household work (including nursing and child care) and work allocated through labor markets, feminist economics is also concerned with gender roles as they relate to economic development and industrialization, and national income accounting.

the neoclassical paradigm, but which, at the same time, had clear relevance to what was developed within the radical paradigms. Nonradical analyses of economic decision making based on the previously noted notions of historical time, ignorance, and nonprobablistic uncertainty are illustrations.[6] Traditional analyses undertaken by nonradicals often had a more liberal and methodological flavor than those emanating from the economics establishment.[7] And nonradical dissent from the neoclassical paradigm also found a home and flourished in this environment.[8]

6. For example, D.W. Katzner, *Time, Ignorance, and Uncertainty in Economic Models* (Ann Arbor: University of Michigan Press, 1998), and D. Vickers, *Economics and the Antagonism of Time: Time, Uncertainty, and Choice in Economic Theory* (Ann Arbor: Univesity of Michigan Press, 1994).

Historical time is the time that human beings actually experience, in which past, present, and future events each have their own time-related characteristics. In neoclassical economics, which abstracts from those characteristics, the only relevant aspect of time has to do with the manner in which it sequences events—one set of events comes before the set of events that follows. In reference to the characteristics of events in historical time, whereas past events have gone by and can never reappear in the same way again, and whereas present events represent current experience, future events are both unknown and unknowable. In light of the ignorance of the future, it is not possible to predict, in the formal or analytic sense of the word, future events, even in probabilistic terms. (The neoclassical approach to time permits and assumes sufficient information availability about the future to allow the determination of probabilities and their use in prediction.) However, surprise is a notion that does not require knowledge of the future and can be invoked by individuals as part of the process of making decisions. It is the characteristics of surprise and its employment in place of probability in economic decision making that is analyzed and explored in the works cited here.

7. For example, D.W. Katzner, *An Introduction to the Economic Theory of Market Behavior* (Cheltenham: Elgar, 2006).

8. See D. Vickers, *The Tyranny of the Market: A Critique of Theoretical Foundations* (Ann Arbor: University of Michigan Press, 1995) and D.W. Katzner, "The Misuse of Measurement in Economics," *Metroeconomica* 49 (1998), pp. 1–22. The latter has been reprinted as Essay 8 in D.W. Katzner, *Unmeasured Information and the Methodology of Social Scientific Inquiry* (Boston: Kluwer, 2001).

The first of these references criticizes neoclassical economics in considerable detail for its avoidance of historical time and ignorance and its use of probability in the analysis of markets and the decision-making behavior of individual consumers and firms. (See immediately preceding note 6.) The second reference describes the kinds of things that render analytical conclusions meaningless when, as is so common in neoclassical economics, variables that are unmeasurable or as yet unmeasured are treated either as if they were at least cardinally quantified, or are replaced by proxy variables that are at least cardinally quantified and taken

Part of the reason for the emergence of the intellectual ethos just described has been indicated in Chapter 1. To recapitulate it here, recall that, due to the restrictiveness of the standards for judging scholarship imposed by the economics establishment, the radicals were unable to publish their research in many of the standard economics journals. Thus, within the Economics Department, publication in nonestablishment-approved outlets was considered to have the same status as publication in approved locations. Because this was Department policy that applied to all faculty equally, a vast array of new research possibilities was opened up to nonradical as well as radical faculty. Combined with the intense intellectual interaction and questioning that went on across paradigms, work related to but outside of the four main paradigms, and work by nonradicals that was critical of the neoclassical paradigm found a comfortable home.

In contrast to the American economics profession, which, as indicated in Chapter 4, had moved politically and ideologically to the right, the University of Massachusetts's Amherst campus Economics Department, even without the strong 1970s comparative paradigmatic emphasis, has maintained its position on the left. Its stress on comparing paradigms has been replaced by a focus on empirical studies and policy analysis. But unlike the profession in general, which currently relies on the functioning of markets to solve problems and improve human lives, the Departmental approach is more inclined to give relatively greater weight to state or governmental intervention. That perspective can be thought of, in part, as an outgrowth of the Keynesianism, liberalism, and radicalism of the 1960s and appears to be more in tune with policies undertaken to

---

to fully represent and provide the same information as the replaced variable. The same reference also shows how alike meaninglessness arises when ordinally measured variables are treated in a similar fashion.

resolve the economic difficulties that began to affect the U.S. and global economies in 2008. Leading the way in this regard is the Political Economy Research Institute (PERI) which was created in 1998. PERI is an independent unit on the Amherst campus of the University of Massachusetts with close ties to the Economics Department. It shares staff and collaborates with Department faculty, and employs and provides fellowships for Department graduate students. Its mission is to develop "workable policy proposals that are capable of improving life on our planet."

In the spring of 2002, the Economics Department was evaluated once again by an outside visiting committee, this time consisting of Keith B. Griffin (University of California at Riverside), William A. Darity, Jr. (University of North Carolina at Chapel Hill and Duke University), and Deidre N. McCloskey (University of Illinois at Chicago).[9] The April report of the external evaluation committee stated in its introduction that:

> The Department of Economics is a jewel in the crown of the University of Massachusetts at Amherst. It is distinctive in that it is one of a very few departments in the country that gives a strong voice to heterodox economics alongside of orthodox economics. Thus it stands out from the bland uniformity of the large majority of economics departments in the United States...in systematically exposing orthodox economics to the competition of ideas...and [thereby] plays a very important role in this country's economics profession.
>
> The Department...has a highly distinguished faculty working within several different traditions in economics [including] Marxian, post-Keynesian, institutionalist, historical, non-Marxian

---

9. There have been other outside evaluations since 1981. This is one of the more recent ones.

radical political economy, and feminist economics. Many members of the faculty enjoy national and international reputations for the quality, originality and relevance of their work. It is no exaggeration to say that the quality of the economics faculty at U Mass [sic] is the envy of other departments which provide a home for heterodox economics.

Finally, the Department is impressive for its diversity, in several dimensions. Its methodological approach is of course diverse.... Many different schools of thought are represented and students, both undergraduates and graduates, are exposed to many different points of view and encouraged to come to their own conclusions.

So it appears that in its descent from the near perfection it enjoyed from the mid-1970s to the mid-1980s, the Economics Department of the University of Massachusetts at Amherst has not, apart from the characteristics that are a direct consequence of that near perfection itself, lost very much. Over the years it has matured into a sort of conscience on the left for tshe economics profession at large, and is unlikely to give up that role soon.

APPENDIX A

Time Line

APPENDIX A

The Transition

September, 1971   Simon Rottenberg joins the Department as head.

Fall, 1971   Rottenberg denies Samuel S. Bowles a visiting appointment in the Economics Department, and Bowles accepts a visiting appointment in the University's Labor Center.

Spring, 1972   Rottenberg refuses to reappoint Best and is overridden by the administration. Rottenberg immediately resigns as Department head.

July, 1972   Alfange is appointed acting head of the Economics Department.

September, 1972   Bowles takes up his visiting appointment in the Labor Center.

Fall, 1972   Bowles is denied tenure by the Harvard Economics Department and Alfange begins to discuss the hiring of the radical package (Bowles, Richard C. Edwards, Herbert Gintis, Steven A. Resnick, Richard D. Wolff) with him.

Winter, 1973   Economists included in the radical package meet in Ashfield.

Spring, 1973   All members of the radical package are hired along with Leonard A. Rapping. Norman D. Aitken is appointed as Economics Department chair to replace acting head Alfange.

The First Three Years

September, 1973   Edwards, Resnick, Wolff, and Rapping all join the Economics Department. Both Smith and Sonnenschein have left.

1973–1974 year   Economics Graduate Student Organization (EGSO) is created.

September, 1974   James R. Crotty, Gintis, and Bowles join the Department.

1974–1975 year   Economics Department delegates the responsibility for assigning teaching assistants to courses to EGSO.

Fight over the granting of tenure to Che S. Tsao and Arthur W. Wright.

Spring, 1975   Donald W. Katzner is appointed and joins the Department in September of that year.

Spring, 1976   Aitken submits his resignation as Department chair. Chair search committee develops a blueprint for overcoming tensions between radicals and non-radicals, including the rule that at most 40% of the Department faculty could be radical, and recommends that Katzner replace Aitken as chair.

Learning to Live Together

September, 1976   Katzner becomes Department chair.

Fall, 1976   Fight over replacement of Department's head clerk.

Fall, 1977   Fight over proper behavior of teaching assistants in courses to which they are assigned.

Spring, 1978   Attack on Marxist emphasis in Departmental teaching by the acting dean of the School of Business Administration.

Fall, 1978   Fight over advertising the Department's PhD program in the *Boston Globe.*

1978–1979 year   Visiting committee reviews and evaluates the Department's PhD program, and the ensuing political attack by the acting dean of the Graduate School is based on a misrepresentation of their report.

August, 1981   Departure of Katzner from the Departmental chair position.

Epilogue

Spring, 1991   De-emphasis of cross-paradigmatic comparisons in the Department's PhD program.

Spring, 1994   Repeal of the Department's radical/nonradical classification scheme and its 40% rule.

APPENDIX B

Heterodox Economics at
Three Other Universities

It is interesting to compare the experience in reference to radical political economics at the University of Massachusetts at Amherst with that in economics departments at other universities. Now, as has been pointed out earlier in this book, the PhD program in the Economics Department on the Amherst campus of the University of Massachusetts was unique from the early 1970s through the mid 1980s in its single-minded, intense focus on radical political economics. PhD programs in economics departments at other universities having radical political economists on their faculties were more generally heterodox in character. (The phrase *heterodox economics* has been recently introduced to refer to approaches to economic thought and analysis that are considered to lie outside of the purview of mainstream economics, or what is taken to be economics by the economics establishment. Currently, radical political economics as defined in Chapter 1, including Marxian economics, along with such fields as post-Keynesian economics, institutional economics, and feminist economics are deemed to fall under the heterodox rubric.) In perusing the following descriptions of contrasting departments, this distinction between the tightly focused PhD program in the University of Massachusetts Department and the more diverse avenues of thought present in the PhD programs in other departments should be kept in mind. Experiences in economics departments at three universities — the University of California at Riverside, the University of Notre Dame, and the New School for Social Research — are presented only in very brief outline with many details omitted.[1] In the first instance, the heterodox group still sits uneasily with an establishment group; in the second, the heterodox group was recently disbanded by the university administration; and in

1. Except as noted, the descriptions that follow were provided (subject to my editing) by, respectively, Steven E. Cullenberg, David F. Ruccio, and Anwar M. Shaikh.

the third, the department has always been comfortably heterodox in overall character. Because, with respect to the third, the Economics Department at the New School has, since its inception, been devoted to the development of various avenues of heterodox economics, it will be useful, in what follows, to trace somewhat more fully the historical development of that department's academic programs than what is presented in the other cases.

University of California at Riverside   At the University of California Riverside, the graduate PhD program in economics was administered in a tricameral way. There were three distinct groups of economists on campus who were involved: (1) those who were in the Economics Department and who were, by the late 1980s, all heterodox economists (not necessarily Marxist or radical political economists) in various ways, (2) those in the School of Business Administration who were establishment or mainstream economists specializing to a considerable extent in econometrics and microeconomic and macroeconomic theory, and (3) a small group of environmental economists located in the Environmental Studies Department and who were also mainstream economists. Policy decisions about curriculum in the economics PhD program were decided by a vote, where each group (not each economist) had one vote. Because the business school and environmental economists voted in the same way on important curricular decisions, they would always defeat the heterodox economists in the Economics Department who had the largest number of faculty constituting in most years a slight majority of all participating economists. This was an unstable situation that led to considerable tension, struggling, and bad feelings, particularly in relation to the nature of the core courses in the economics PhD program. Circumstances changed in 1992, when the economists from the business school were merged with those in the Economics Department. The environmental economists remained outside of the Department and continued to offer courses in the PhD program, but they no longer voted on matters relating to it. Although the governance structure became more democratic with one faculty member now having one vote, the battle over the core courses has persisted. To this day the core is still a very mainstream sequence of courses.

University of Notre Dame   At the University of Notre Dame, the history of the Department of Economics as a department open to different perspectives (consisting of both mainstream and heterodox theories and approaches) began in 1975 when Charles Wilber was hired away from American University to serve as the chair of the Notre Dame department. Wilber and subsequent chairs worked to keep that tradition alive, in both the undergraduate and graduate programs. Over the years, the Department focused on key areas, such as economic development, labor, history of economic thought, and public policy that were not necessarily cultivated in mainstream economics departments. It also included, in addition to main-stream theory and methods, a wide range of theories (including Marxian, post-Keynesian, and institutionalist economics) and methods (including case studies, history, and textual interpretation). The rationale of the department as one that was open to divergent theories and methods was twofold: It served as an alternative to programs that were purely mainstream in nature, and it corresponded to the Catholic character at Notre Dame, especially in emphasizing the heterodox issues of economic and social justice.

Beginning in the 1980s, the Department came under pressure from the university administration to become more mainstream. The Department successfully resisted that pressure until, in 2003, the administration decided to split the Department by creating a new department of economics devoted solely to neoclassical economics that was called the Department of Economics and Econometrics (with five faculty), and to rename the existing department as the Department of Economics and Policy Studies (with sixteen faculty). The administration also decreed that the economics PhD program and all subsequent faculty hires in economics and would go to the new department, and the renamed department was barred from obtaining new faculty and from participating in the doctoral program. Then, in February of 2010, the university administration dissolved the Department of Economics and Policy Studies, scattered its faculty elsewhere in the University, and renamed the mainstream department the Department of Economics.

New School for Social Research The New School for Social Research[2] was founded in 1919 by a distinguished group of intellectuals, some of whom were teaching at Columbia University in New York City during the World War I. Fervent pacifists, they took a public stand against the war and were censured by the Columbia's president. The outspoken professors responded by resigning from Columbia and later opening up their own university for adults in New York's Chelsea district as a place where people could exchange ideas freely with scholars and artists representing a wide range of intellectual, aesthetic, and political orientations. The original faculty included Charles A. Beard, Thorstein B. Veblen, James Harvey Robinson, Wesley Clair Mitchell, John Dewey, and Alvin S. Johnson.

With unorthodox economists like Veblen, Robinson, and Mitchell on the faculty, it is not surprising that the history of heterodox economics in the Economics Department extends back to the very beginning of the New School. An influx from Germany and France in the 1930s brought a new group of progressive (and unorthodox) European scholars into the

2. This paragraph was taken from the New School's web site.

picture: Adolph Lowe, Hans P. Neisser, Gerhard Colm, Jacob Marschak, Emil Lederer, Hans Staudinger, Eduard Heimann, and Abba P. Lerner were among the foreign economists who arrived at the New School at that time.[3] John Maynard Keynes, visiting from England, lectured in the Department in 1931, and Franco Modigliani, an Italian student, received his doctorate under Marschak's supervision in 1944.

This phase lasted into the 1960s, at which point a different heterodox current began to appear in the Department through the interests of faculty members Robert L. Heilbroner, Michael Hudson, and Stephen H. Hymer. That current was an American-grown tradition, which, in part, made the history of thought central to the Department, and focused on the United States in a global context. Edward J. Nell added an important Keynesian and Cambridge (UK) link, which has been maintained to the present day. The long-standing European connections noted earlier were extended to Italy in keeping with the economic debates of the times. Anwar M. Shaikh, David Gordon, and Ross Thomson brought radical and Marxian economics to the Department in the early 1970s, Willi Semmler added a strong mathematical orientation in the early 1980s, and, during the same period, Heidi Hartmann, Gita Sen, Nancy Folbre, and Rhonda M. Williams made gender and race central to the curriculum. There was also a corresponding change in the student body, whose composition shifted toward the Third World, with a strong representation of Turks, Iranians, Mexicans, and Brazilians. The political struggles across the world were reflected in the Economics Department in lively theoretical debates between Keynesians, Marxians, neo-Ricardians, and institutionalists.

However, by the late 1980s, the rapidly rising net cost of a New School education significantly shrank the international (and more radical) component of the student body. At the same time, the Department came under increasing pressure from the administration to change. Gender and race substantially vanished as a field of study. In keeping with the times, mathematics, microeconomics, game theory, and econometrics became more important, and history of economic thought and Marxian economics correspondingly less so. But international trade, economic development, and Keynesian theory remained central throughout, and they were strengthened by the arrival of William S. Milberg and Lance Taylor in the 1990s. John L. Eatwell reinforced the Cambridge view and connection during that time. He was also instrumental in forming the Center for Economic Policy

Analysis (CEPA) near the end of the period, with the aim of furthering alternative perspectives on global economic policy. Duncan K. Foley's arrival in the early 2000s greatly enhanced the offerings in game theory, microeconomics, and agent-based simulation. On the other hand, what had been a full two-year graduate sequence in Reading and Using Marx's *Capital*, which ran for two decades, essentially disappeared from the curriculum by the end of the 1990s. However, these themes remain alive, albeit in reduced form, in seminars and occasional courses by Shaikh and Foley. In recent times, the student interest in them seems to have reawakened. Most recently, Teresa Ghilarducci joined the Department as the head of the Schwartz Center for Policy Analysis (formerly the CEPA) in the mid-2000s, reorienting its focus on U.S. concerns in a global context. Finally, the program in economic development and international inequality have been particularly strengthened through the arrival of Sanjay Reddy and Lopamudra Banerjee.

INDEX

Humphrey, H.H., 58
Humphries, J., 130 n. 4
Hunsberger, I.M., 82, 83, 84, 85, 87, 99
Hymer, S.H., 190

Ideal university, 6–7
    and perfection, 7
Ignorance, 153, 178
Interaction, economics faculty and
    graduate students, 16–18, 21,
    171–172
    among radical faculty, 127–128
    radical-nonradical, 17–18, 152–155
Interferences by state in operations, 43
    creation and dissolution of Board of
    Regents, 41
    merger with state bureaucracy, 34
Invasion, "guerilla", 168

Johnson, A.S., 189
Johnson, L.B., 52, 54, 66, 67

Katzner, D.W., 14 n. 25, 15,
    18 n. 30, 145
    appointment to chair position, 149
    departure from chair
    position, 168–169
    hiring of, 144
    interactions with
    radicals, 17–18, 153–155
    research of, 153–155, 178 nn. 6–8
    and teaching microeconomic
    theory, 17–18, 145–146
    threat of resignation from chair
    position, 160
    uneasiness in the chair position, 151
Kendrick, D., 77 n. 16
Kennedy, J.F., 66, 115 n.10
Keynes, J.M., 10 n. 17, 12, 63, 190
Kindahl, J.K., 10, 15, 84, 85, 86, 88,
    89, 90 n. 10, 92, 102, 113 n. 6,
    120, 121, 122, 123, 140,
    164, 176

conflict over Best
    reappointment, 97–99, 101–102
conflict with Department, 95–96, 101
conflict with Department over
    status as head, 91–92
plans for Department, 85–87
replacement as head, 105–106
resignation from head position,
    99–100
King, E.J., 41
King, M.L., 49, 50, 51, 77
Klein, L.R., 83, 94
Kuhn, T., 7

Land-grant colleges, 28
Larcom, R.C., 36
Lederer, E., 190
Lederle, J.W., 40
Lee, F., xi, 70 n. 7, 174 n. 3
Lerner, A.J., 1, 3, 171
Lerner, A.P., 190
Levine, D., 70
Lévy-Garboua, L., 154
Lifschultz, L.S., 24, 70 n. 8
Lincoln, A., 28
Lowe, A., 190
Lowe, F., 1, 3, 171
Lucas, R.E., Jr., 121, 133

Marschak, J., 190
Marshall, A., 76 n. 15
Martin, T.J., 55 n. 2, 59 n. 5
Marx, K., 10, 79, 115 n. 10, 120,
    172, 191
Marxism combined with Keynesian
    macroeconomics, 12–13, 15
Marxism combined with political and
    social liberalism, 12, 15
Marxism as mutual interaction of all
    analytical elements, 13–15
Massachusetts Agricultural
    College, 27–35
    and admission of women, 32, 34